Charles Henry Parkhurst, William Howe Telman

Municipal Reform Movements in the United States

Charles Henry Parkhurst, William Howe Telman

Municipal Reform Movements in the United States

ISBN/EAN: 9783337295370

Printed in Europe, USA, Canada, Australia, Japan

Cover: Foto ©ninafisch / pixelio.de

More available books at **www.hansebooks.com**

THE TEXT-BOOK OF THE NEW REFORMATION

MUNICIPAL REFORM MOVEMENTS IN THE UNITED STATES

BY

WILLIAM HOWE TOLMAN, Ph.D.

SECRETARY OF THE CITY VIGILANCE LEAGUE, NEW-YORK

WITH AN INTRODUCTORY CHAPTER BY THE

REV. CHARLES H. PARKHURST, D. D.

PRESIDENT OF THE CITY VIGILANCE LEAGUE, NEW-YORK

FLEMING H. REVELL COMPANY
NEW-YORK   CHICAGO   TORONTO
1895

TO MY MOTHER
THIS BOOK IS DEDICATED
BY HER SON
IN LOVING RECOGNITION OF HER
INSPIRATION TO NOBLE IDEALS
OF MANHOOD.

PREFACE

THERE are very few municipalities in our country where a reform movement would have no reason for existence. Too often, however, the mention of a reform movement conveys the idea of destruction, an immense amount of tearing down, so that it has come to pass that the so-called practical reformer is almost as much dreaded as the practical politician. On the other hand, it is true that many a reform must tear down, in order that the ground may be prepared for the superstructure of improved conditions; but it is also a fact that certain reforms, destined to accomplish permanent results, are expending their utmost energies on the constructive phases of their work. To illustrate concretely: the recent action of the London County Council in insuring the lives of all the workmen who are engaged in the dangerous parts of the work of constructing the tunnel under the Thames is a reform in the right direction, and there are organizations that are striving to secure an increasing regard for the claims of life, in preference to those of property. The differences in the two phases of reform may again be illustrated by the work of the Society for the Prevention of Crime and of the City Vigilance League, the efforts of the former being along *de*structive and of the latter along *con*structive lines.

The spirit of reform is now manifesting itself in a great diversity of organizations, based on the fundamental principle that municipal affairs must be administered in the interests of all the citizens—not merely the taxpayers, but also the non-taxpayers, because the latter as well as the former must dwell in our cities, and intend to make them their civic home. One theory of municipal administration holds that a city is simply a civic household, and the more closely it approximates a well ordered and appointed individual home the nearer it approaches ideal conditions. On this point the Committee of Seventy laid particular stress, and it is safe to assume that the voters indorsing its demands responded because of the high standard of the following ante-election statement: "The call goes to the citizens of New York to face the dangers that confront them, and resolutely to determine that these conditions shall cease and that the affairs of the city shall henceforth be conducted as a well-ordered, efficient, and economical household, in the interests of the health, comfort, and safety of the people." After the enunciation of the theory of its demands for civic betterment, the Committee then enumerated the *positive* measures necessary to secure it: it demanded that the quality of the Public Schools be improved; that Small Parks be opened in the densely populated parts of the city; Rapid Transit; that adequate Public Baths and Lavatories be provided; that the Docks and Water-front be improved; and that the Street-cleaning be thorough.

In the desire of effecting an organization for municipal reform there is great danger that both time and energy are wasted, because either the society in question is not adapted to local needs or fails to respond to the demands that are made upon it. These difficulties might easily have been obviated if the founders had made a more careful study of the local conditions, or if they had utilized the experiences of similar societies in other cities that were grappling with the same problems. If this had been done a working constitution could have been framed that would have secured all the objects of the organization in question. To illustrate: St. Paul may use as a model a Philadelphia society, which will not work at all in the Western city, but admirably serves its purpose in Philadelphia.

It is therefore the object of this book to bring together, for comparison and selection, the salient and essential points in all the leading reform movements, in order that any persons desirous of forming a new organization may have a knowledge of those methods which the successful experience of other communities has commended. The great need in municipal reform is a kind of Reform Clearing House where the various plans and methods of work might be reported, in order that ways and means may be carefully studied. Then a composite constitution can be framed, which may be worked at once, whereby valuable time and effort will be utilized from the very start. There are also numerous movements not so much for municipal reform as for what may be called civic betterment. The varied phases of these organizations have been described in the methods of some one typical society. Any summary of the elements in successful reform organizations would be sadly incomplete without the mention of women's work. Particularly was this true in Brooklyn in 1893, and in New York in 1894. Accordingly one part has been devoted to the work of the women in municipal reform.

In the last part the work of the City Vigilance League has been described in detail, because it stands as a kind of object-lesson of what may be accomplished in the constructive work of civic reform. Its methods are of value because only such have been retained as were clearly shown to have stood the test of experience. In its early days it had no definite policy nor any delicately constructed theories. Its working capital was the knowledge that New York City must be made better, and it undertook the contract. In the words of its founder, "Our sole aim is to raise the tone of our citizenship. Whatever concerns the welfare of our city is made the subject of inquiry and conference." Because the League was confined to no one method it has made use of all, retaining those which best serve its purposes. However, it must be carefully noted that even its administrative methods should not be followed without a careful adaptation to local needs.

TABLE OF CONTENTS

                                                                            PAGE

INTRODUCTORY CHAPTER BY THE REV. CHARLES H. PARKHURST, D.D. 15

PART I.—THE CIVIC RENAISSANCE................... 27

THE FUNCTIONS OF THE CITY:
    The Disciplinary and the Regulative, 27.
    The Sanitary, 28.
    The Recreative, 28.
    The Educational, 28.
    The Functional, 28.
    The Curative and the Reformatory, 28.

THE CAUSES OF THE AWAKENING:
    The Moral, 30.
    Non-Partizanship, 34.
    Hatred of Bosses, 35.
    Insistence on the Positive and Constructive, 38.
    The Union of the Forces of Good Citizenship, 40.

IMPORTANCE OF THE VICTORY BECAUSE WON IN NEW YORK.

CAUSES OF ENCOURAGEMENT:
    The Organization of the Young People's Societies in the Churches for Good Citizenship, 42.
    The Fact of the Awakened Civic Conscience, 41.

HOW TO UTILIZE THE VICTORY:
    The Creation of a Municipal Council, Elected by the People, hence having Official Sanction, 41.
    Increased Educational Facilities in Citizenship, 42.
    The Inducement of a Civic Ideal, 43.
    The Subordination of the Commercial and Material to the Social and Progressive Spirit, 43.
    A Positive or Constructive, Rather than a Negative or Destructive Program, 44.

PART II.—MUNICIPAL REFORM MOVEMENTS 47

The Advance Club, Providence, 47.
American Institute of Civics, New York, 48.
Anti-Spoils League, New York, 49.
The Citizens' Association of Albany, 50.
Citizens' Association of Boston, 52.
The Citizens' Association, Buffalo, 55.
The Citizens' Association of Chicago, 56.
Citizens' Club, Cincinnati, 58.
The Citizens' Federation of Toledo, 59.
Citizens' League, Camden, 60.
Citizens' League of New Rochelle, 61.
The Citizens' League of the Town of Norwalk, 62.
Citizens' Municipal Association of Philadelphia, 64.
The Citizens' Municipal League, Bridgeton, 65.
The Citizens' Protective Association, New Orleans, 67.
City Club of Hartford, 68.
City Club of New Brunswick, 69.
The City Club of New York, 70.
Committee of Public Safety, Troy, 71.
The City Government Club, Pittsburg, 72.
City Improvement Society, New York, 73.
City Reform Club, New York, 75.
The Civic Club, Beloit, 75.
The Civic Federation of Chicago, 77.
The Civic Federation of Detroit, 79.
Civic Federation of Galesburg, 80.
Committee of Fifty, Albany, 81.
Committee of Public Safety, St. Louis, 82.
Committee of Seventy, New York, 85.
Council of Confederated Good Government Clubs, New York, 91.
Good Government Club A, New York, 93.
Good Government Clubs, 95.
The Good Citizenship Educational League of Omaha, 96.
Good Government Club of Berkeley, 97.
Good Government Club of Yonkers, 99.
The International Law and Order League, Boston, 100.
Citizens' Law and Order League, New Haven, 101.
The Library Hall Association of Cambridge, 101.
Massachusetts Society for Promoting Good Citizenship, Boston, 103.

The Men's Patriotic Guild, Pittsburg, 104.
Municipal Association, Champaign, 105.
Municipal Club of Decatur, 106.
Municipal Club of Rochester, 107.
Municipal Improvement Association of Kansas City, 108.
The Municipal League of Grand Rapids, 110.
The Municipal League of Milwaukee, 112.
The Municipal League of Omaha, 114.
The Municipal League of Philadelphia, 115.
The Municipal League, Schenectady, 116.
Municipal Reform Club, Syracuse, 117.
The Municipal League of Boston, 119.
National Civil-Service Reform League, New York, 121.
National Municipal League, Philadelphia, 122.
The Reform League, Baltimore, 124.
The Social Reform Club, New York, 128.
Society for the Prevention of Crime, New York, 129.
The Trades League of Philadelphia, 131.

PART III.—MOVEMENTS FOR CIVIC BETTERMENT... 137

The American Institute of Christian Sociology, New York, 139.
The Altrurian League, New York, 140.
Better Dwellings Society, Boston, 141.
The Brotherhood of the Kingdom, New York, 142.
The Charity Organization Society of the City of New York, 145.
The Institutional Church, 147.
Municipal Labor Bureaus, 150.
The Municipal Program Conferences, New York, 152.
The Social Settlement, 154.
The Young People's Society of Christian Endeavor, Boston, 158.
The Christian Citizenship League, Chicago, 159.
Union for Practical Progress, 161.
Union for Public Good, Baltimore, 162.

PART IV.—WOMEN'S WORK IN MUNICIPAL REFORM. 167

The Civic Club of Philadelphia, 168.
The Civitas Club, Brooklyn, 169.
Ladies' Health Protective Association, New York, 171.
The Municipal Order League of Chicago, 171.

Philadelphia Branch of the National Women's Health Protective Association, 173.
Women's Health Protective Association of Brooklyn, 174.
Civic League (originally Woman's Municipal League), New York, 176.
The Society for Political Study, New York, 180.

PART V.—THE CITY VIGILANCE LEAGUE............ 183

ITS ORIGIN, GROWTH, OBJECT, ADMINISTRATIVE POLICY, AND METHODS.

FACTS FOR THE TIMES

BY

CHARLES H. PARKHURST, D.D.

Of all the cities in America, our problem is the most stupendous, our example the most exalted, our opportunity the most august. We should be weighted, not with the sense of our importance, but with the burden of our duties. Above all, we should love our city. We should be proud of its unparalleled advantages, of its splendid history. Unexampled for situation; enthroned at the gate of the New World; with seas and bays spread out like carpets at her feet, and imperial rivers wrapped about her like garments; armed with power and crowned with beauty; rich in the memory and the living presence of worthy citizens: statesmen, soldiers, poets, philanthropists, preachers, inventors, explorers, financeers, merchants—her history, her fame, her might, are fit to thrill the soul and challenge the loyalty of every man and woman within her borders.

The love of city or section above the love of country—above the love, indeed, of humanity—leads to issues contracted and ignoble. I would preach no narrow patriotism; but there is a sense in which it is deeply true that he who serves his city best serves his country best. Fellow-citizens of the metropolis, let us not fail in civic patriotism, in the love and service of this goodly city of our hearts and homes.

RICHARD WATSON GILDER.

INTRODUCTORY CHAPTER

FACTS FOR THE TIMES

By Charles H. Parkhurst, D.D.

The issue of the work by Dr. William Howe Tolman herewith presented affords opportunity for the hasty mention of a number of matters germane to the situation.

1. It is well that it should be understood that the present movement in New York City is first of all a moral movement, and has its grounds in the churches and the synagogues. A very large per cent. of every live current question is ethical in its ingredients, and falls, therefore, naturally and properly, within the jurisdiction of the church. For reasons which it is not easy to understand, the church, while maintaining a certain kind of authority in regard to domestic questions and also in regard to social ones, has betrayed a singular disposition to surrender everything like authority touching questions of civic privilege and duty. This has sprung, doubtless, from a number of causes, one being that the clergy have not, in general, been disposed to assert themselves upon this ground, the training which they have received not having been such as to qualify them to speak either with assurance or with effect. There has prevailed, also, among a good many of the cloth, a spirit of "other-worldliness," which has included a conviction that the prime duty of the church is to fit men and women for the world to come, and also a conviction that there is not

much to be gained by trying to improve the world that is here. In addition to this there is always a disposition, on the part of those that stand out of relation with the church, to resent as unwarranted intermeddling any effort on the part of the church or its ministry to interest themselves in current civic affairs, whether national or municipal. If we say anything in the pulpit about the moral law in its relation to the community or the State, we are charged with preaching politics and with dabbling sensationally in what is none of our business. It is a gratifying fact that earnest citizens, whether in the church or out of the church, show signs of outgrowing this notion of the transcendental sphere of the pulpit, and that they are disposed, in some degree at least, to put themselves under the leadership of the clergy to the degree that the clergy understand themselves and understand the situation, and to the degree, also, that the questions to be discussed are questions of a moral import.

It is also to be mentioned in this connection that a very hopeful sign of the times is to be found in the fact of the rapid growth of Christian Endeavor Societies, especially when it is remembered that good Christian citizenship has recently been laid down as one of the prominent planks in the platform of their organization. A politician has recently remarked of the Christian Endeavor Societies that they promise a complete overturning of the existing order of things, and that the organization will derive no small portion of its influence and effectiveness for good from the fact that it is strictly non-political in its character and intention.

The work of the City Vigilance League illustrates the above principles. We are trying, under the auspices of that society, to develop as large a number as possible of young men who shall concern themselves with the positive interests of our community, and who shall strive to encourage the development among us of all those conditions—intellectual, moral, social, sanitary, and industrial—which shall operate to make New York as fine a town as it is possible for any town to become. Incidentally, of course, we come in conflict with that which is evil, and have to deal with it; but our prime object is not to repress evil possibilities, but to encourage the possibilities of good. We are trying to acquaint our young men, both native and foreign, with our system of municipal government, the elements of administrative machinery. We are encouraging the members of the League to acquaint themselves with the functions exercised by different officers under the municipal government, that so they may be more intelligent in their estimate of the official fitness of candidates. We are studying up the matter of primary-school accommodations with reference to the fact that the city is under solemn obligations to give each child an opportunity to acquire the rudiments of an English education, although at present failing to meet its obligations in that particular. We are instituting along certain lines a comparison between certain sanitary conveniences as afforded in this city —or rather as denied in this city—and as afforded in other cities, especially foreign cities. These are specimens of the lines of work which we are prosecuting. Such lines are of a distinctively constructive character, and although our organization has been in existence but a little while, we know that one effect that has already been produced by it has been to qualify the members of the League to estimate more intelligently our existing municipal conditions, and therefore to qualify them to take more intelligent steps looking to the betterment of those conditions.

2. No one can appreciate our municipal situation as it exists at the date of this writing (February, 1895) without understanding that the victory which was gained last November was but the first step toward a long series of victories requiring still to be gained before we attain to anything like the perfection of municipal government. Politicians work three

hundred and sixty-five days in the year. Men interested in civic matters, but outside of the political circles, are apt to be fairly well satisfied with themselves if they work two or three weeks of the year. The consequence is that when a positive victory has been gained the indefatigable politicians consider such result rather as the starting-point from which a new term of effort is to be put forth, while the rest of us are very likely inclined to feel that it is the resting-point at which our efforts are to be intermitted.

There is at the present time in New York a phenomenal amount of just thinking and sincere desire along the lines of civic amelioration; but it is a fact that has to be conceded that honest intention misses its purposes except as it is organized and equipped with the appliances for making its purposes actual. The question naturally suggests itself whether it is not going to be necessary, in order to the permanence of non-partizan city administration, to have an organization developed and perfected and furnished with all requisite machinery, that shall be in some respects similar to the appurtenances by means of which, in national matters, the Republican or Democratic party goes to work to achieve its objects. There will be the continual intrusion of national politics into municipal concerns until there has been built up a municipal organization sufficiently earnest to discourage such intrusion, and sufficiently compact and efficient to neutralize and to render impossible all such intrusion. The theory of city government heretofore has been that it is simply State government localized at a specific point. The contest which we have before us will have for its object to establish more distinctly and definitely the municipal organism as being in essential (not superficial) particulars distinct from the State organism. According as that idea becomes distinctly defined, recognized, and adopted, the possibility becomes enhanced of building up, inside of the city, an association which shall be the corporate expression of the principles upon which our recent victory was based, namely, non-partizanship and the maintenance of municipal administration on distinctively business principles.

No one can contemplate our present situation without experiencing solicitude as to the events that will transpire when the present mayoralty term is finished. The margin of our victory was numerically so small that a subtraction of twenty-five thousand from the number of those who combined to elect Mr. Strong could easily throw the city back again into the hands of Tammany Hall. It is probable that some considerable number of those who were influential in defeating Tammany last autumn engaged in the struggle for revenue purposes, and who, if they had foreseen with accuracy that their selfish intentions were to be thwarted, would quite as readily have thrown in their influence with the very party that they antagonized. In this statement we have no specific persons in mind; but it is one of those things that can so easily be true that it is presumable that it is true. The organizing power of boodle is immense, but only so long as there is boodle. Now all these contingencies require to be taken into the account and to have due emphasis laid upon them in estimating the probable outcome three years hence. If we are going to have an honest city government as a permanency we are not going to be able to depend upon the sporadic honesty and civic virtue of people who are unorganized. This is one of those considerations that need to be thrown into the air in order that men's thoughts may be set at work upon them, and in order that our earnest citizenship may crystallize around some policy which shall make our present municipal condition something more than a mere break between two eras of municipal corruption.

3. The contest immediately in hand in this city has to do with the destruction of political despotism. We have escaped

from under the dominion of one despot only to be brought under the yoke of another, who, though less corrupt personally, is inspired with the same greed of power and is prolific with quite as large possibilities of mischief. The boss is not a new phenomenon, but has manifested itself in one form or another at every stage of political history. It has simply varied its type to fit the shifting circumstances with which it came into association. In its interior character it is radically alien to the genius of American institutions, and is to be destroyed not so much by being belittled and reprobated as by building up in individual citizens that sense of personal authority and appreciation of personal right and privilege which shall regard "bossism" as an impertinent intrusion upon personal prerogatives. In this, as in every other line of improvement, the scriptural maxim obtains that the "evil must be overcome by the good."

There is no more of the spirit of dictator in the individual who is now trying to administer the affairs of this city and State in the interests of himself and his henchmen than there has been in his Tammany predecessor; and the reason why he is being more bitterly antagonized is that there is at the present time among the rank and file of our citizens an aroused sense that each individual citizen counts for something, or ought to count for something; and the most direct method of making this warfare continuous until it issues in victory over "bossism" of all types is to go on stimulating the sense of authority possessed by the citizen, until there be a general realization that "bossism" is an insult done to citizenship. It must be remembered, however, that the burden of accountability is not to be laid upon the "boss" alone, but upon the creatures that are contented to be used as his implements and tools. The "boss" by himself is powerless. The case is something as in arithmetic, where the integer 1, for instance, is the lowest unit of value; but it becomes 10 if it has associated with it a zero at its right hand. Now the tool is the zero which multiplies the integer-boss by ten, and, without having any value of its own to speak of, multiplies inordinately the individual value of the integer which it serves; so that while we direct our warfare in the first instance against the "boss," we must not neglect to put the bulk of our reprobation into our treatment of the political zeros who are contented to serve him and to multiply ten, one hundred, or a thousand fold his individual significance and power.

These are lessons that require to be reiterated, and to be made part of the civic creed of our rising young citizenship.

I

THE CIVIC RENAISSANCE

Innumerable are the evils engendered in the body politic by this worship of gain, and the substitution of material in place of moral ideals of the commonwealth. The high ideals of patriotism are dethroned. Young men of ability scorn to serve the commonwealth, and seek to satisfy their ambitions in the more lucrative pursuits of business. Which shall be blamed most severely for the confessed evils of our day, the vices of the illiterate and degraded who fill the slums of our metropolis, or the selfish indifference and the blind, ease-loving optimism of the more opulent classes, who neglect the social obligations which are the just concomitants of the social privileges which they enjoy, and grow faithless to the democratic institutions whose beneficent shelter has furnished the smooth channels and broad highways for their commercial aggrandizement? I leave this question for others to answer; I simply reaffirm the ideals on which our grand commonwealth is built, and which are now too often overlooked or ignored. The principle of democracy has not failed. The people may still be trusted. From the people ill informed we may still appeal, with high confidence of success, to the people better informed.

Social well-being, not the mere aggregation of wealth, is the chief aim of government and the criterion of its successful administration.

LEIGHTON WILLIAMS.

MUNICIPAL REFORM MOVEMENTS

I

THE CIVIC RENAISSANCE

By way of introduction it is necessary that we have a clear idea of the functions of the municipality, for as we answer the following question our municipal horizon will be broad or narrow. Is a city government organized for the purpose of enriching the present political party and a favored set of contractors, or is it the opportunity for the broadest development of the people —you and I, we who live above Fourteenth Street, as well as the Italian of the "Bend" and of "Little Italy," the Chinaman of Mott Street, the Jew of Hester Street, and the African of Thompson Street (for all these are among the component parts of our municipality)? Let us, therefore, very briefly enumerate the functions of the modern city, those details which must be administered twelve months in the year and twenty-four hours in each day, whoever may chance to fill the municipal offices, or however poorly they may do their work:

1. THE DISCIPLINARY AND THE REGULATIVE, included under the policing of the city and all those relations in which the citizen cannot do as he pleases, but must yield a certain part of his rights to the welfare of the whole.

2. The Sanitary, included under the subject of housing, inspection of homes and workshops, compulsory vaccination, the prevention of contagious diseases, and the inspection of breadstuffs.

3. The Recreative: parks, playgrounds (particularly in connection with the public schools), music, and theaters.

4. The Educational: the public schools, kindergartens, technical and manual-training schools, schools for science, art, and music, museums and libraries.

5. The Functional, or the means of carrying on the necessary life of the city. Under this head are included paving and the care of the streets, transportation of all kinds, the water and gas supply, sewerage, and the preparing of new or annexed districts as the municipality becomes congested.

6. The Curative and the Reformatory, included under the provision of asylums and hospitals for the insane, the deaf, dumb, and blind; prisons and reformatories for the delinquent classes.

Our city is not a business corporation, but is a body politic—a fact which will justify it in doing a great variety of things that are necessary for the completest satisfaction of the requirements of all its component parts. A business corporation would scout at the necessity of many of these, and cut them down as useless expenditures; but not so a body politic that is concerned with the civic welfare of its members. A business corporation has but little concern how its employees live, what kind of food they eat, how they amuse themselves, what they read, or how they try to improve themselves; a municipality must concern itself with these things. Life must be given the precedence over property. Thousands of New York citizens live in the tenements because of what they suppose is the lower rental, and because they must live near their work; large numbers of them live in abodes of one room, and yet greater numbers in two or three roomed dwellings. If private capital will not provide decent accommodations for its tenants, and charges an enormous rental for the accommodation which it does offer, what is there to prevent the city from insisting that the welfare of its denizens must be regarded? Why should it not build municipal baths, wash-houses, and lavatories, so that it can offer satisfaction to needs that are only essential to right living? In the case of the public wash-house the family laundry can be done away from the narrow quarters of the so-called home, at a charge that will pay the running expenses of the establishment and at the same time make the life of the family in question more tolerable. Why should you and I give up certain of our rights to the streets to a company that will supply the means of transportation, but at a rate of fare that yields a splendid revenue to the comparatively few men comprising the corporation? Is there any reason why the people should not say, "This is our city, and these are our streets. We must have adequate transit facilities, but we propose to have them at the lowest cost, and if there is any profit let it go to the community and not to the few. We will do our own transportation if necessary, and if there is a profit we will use it in lowering the fare"? That is exactly what the people of Glasgow did in 1894, and the municipality of that canny Scotch city is now operating its own system of tram-cars. I often think that it was an extremely fortunate circumstance that the government took under its control the business of the post-office, and that it did not fall into the hands of some choice syndicate. In the administrative report of the city of Berlin for the year 1892–93 taxation furnished about one half of the twenty-one million dollars of receipts, and of the remaining eleven millions the profits from the city's gas and water works were five millions. The report also mentioned thirty-nine separate departments, among which were city markets, parks, wash-houses, children's playgrounds, municipal savings-banks and pawnshops, and a vast system of sewerage-farms. London provides municipal lodging-houses, winter swimming-baths, small parks and playgrounds, lavatories, and evening recreation schools, as a matter of course. Now ask yourselves how many of these necessities, to say nothing of the luxuries, of life New York provides for the people? Where will you direct the visiting foreigner who may wish to compare your municipal lodging-houses with those in his own city? What can you point to in the way of a public library, and what is there about our public-school system of which we can be very proud? Are these things any the less needful in New York?

From a calm and impartial survey of the conditions in our cities we are compelled to admit the low tone of the municipal spirit. Who are the men who stand forth as the conspicuous leaders of our great political parties and what are their claims to such preëminence? Does the press mold and shape public opinion, or is it a weathercock that is turned by the prevailing sentiments, instead of being a guide-board pointing out the right road? Have the clergy massed their influence on the side of the forces making for civic righteousness, or have they frittered away their energies in the discussion of the wisdom of methods and policies? To what extent do you allow yourself to be made dissatisfied by the lack of civic spirit, and what effort are you making in helping on the civic renaissance? That there has been a civic awakening is beyond dispute. It will accordingly be of profit to examine the principal causes, so that we can give a reason for the political faith that is in us.

The foremost cause of the civic awakening was moral, for the struggle was clearly fought on moral grounds. In all the campaign speeches of Dr. Parkhurst the trend of thought was that the issues were those of right and wrong, and the planking of his platform was civic righteousness. Before November 6, 1894, the moral blood of the body politic flowed sluggishly; but Dr. Parkhurst injected fresh blood and stiffened the civic system by a vigorous tonic; then the veins pulsated to throbbing, and the new life-bringing energy manifested itself in the arms, legs, and brains of the voters who deposited their ballots at the polls. The civic conscience had been aroused; each individual who acted for good government on election day was possessed of no extra amount of virtue, but used what was already in his possession, with a surprising result in a good many cases, I have no doubt. The editorials of the leading journals on the day following the election reflected primarily the moral issues of the campaign.

"The ten commandments have prevailed by majorities that vindicate the right of the people to rule. No one can measure the practical effect of the votes recorded yesterday." *

"Henceforth let no American citizen ever despair of the Republic or doubt the endurance of representative institutions. Yesterday's magnificent uprising in this city triumphantly delivered popular government from the sneers of its enemies and the fears of its friends. It has long been acknowledged by enlightened minds that the one supreme test of free institutions was in the administration of the affairs of great municipalities. For years New York, oppressed by bossism, degraded by the reign of crime, ruled by the most perfectly disciplined and the most absolutely corrupt political machine ever fashioned by man, has been an object of scorn to the adherents of monarchy and a source of deep humiliation to the upholders of civic freedom. Tammany has seemed omnipotent. . . . Timid men said that its malignant reign could never be overthrown. They forgot the invincible power of right. They did not measure the irresistible might of the awakened American conscience.

"To-day New York is free by the act of her own citizens. The voters of the metropolis have battered down, by their ballots, the political despotism that had plundered them so long,

* *The New York Tribune*, November 7, 1894.

and have proclaimed anew the immortal doctrines of that Declaration of Independence which is the charter of American liberty. Republican government has vindicated itself in the stronghold of its enemies, and triumphed gloriously over obstacles greater than any which it has encountered in the history of the world. For this vindication and this deliverance every loyal American has reason to rejoice with joy unspeakable, to look forward to the future with renewed faith and courage, and to return thanks with all reverence and all sincerity to Almighty God!"*

"Now may the people of this city give themselves up to unbounded jubilation and thanksgiving. New York is redeemed and will be regenerated.

"The battle for good government and public morality has been fought, and a glorious victory won by the people and for the people.

"Tammany has not been beaten simply. Its forces have not been routed merely. It has been crushed, its vicious sway broken, its power annihilated. The ground-swell of popular feeling and might that moved against it with the silent, all-crushing force of an Alpine glacier has swept it to destruction.

"It was a revolution that closes a dark and opens a bright era in the municipal affairs of New York. It marks the downfall of a long reign of riotous abuse which has cursed New York as no other American city has ever been cursed and made the very name of Tammany a synonym throughout the civilized world of corrupt politics, arrogant bossism, and demoralizing misrule. All this the victimized people of New York endured until it was carried beyond the limit of endurance, when they rose in their might and their wrath, and cried in thunder-tones, 'Thus far and no farther!'

"It was a grand uprising, which attests the conscience, the determination, and the power of the people when aroused and

* *The New York Press*, November 7, 1894.

summoned to the rescue of popular government and public morality. It was a glorious victory that will be hailed with joy and acclamation wherever vicious boss rule and official corruption are condemned and honesty in public affairs is approved. . . .

". . . It means, in short, municipal regeneration—that every department of the city government shall be reformed and conducted honestly, efficiently, and economically for the public good." *

The union of the moral forces in the community was magnificently voiced by the clergy of this city about two weeks before the election; but I could have wished that there had been one-hundredth part of this clerical support about two years before, when the few who were fighting in the van of civic reform needed every ounce of support and encouragement. It was then not so respectable to be allied with the reform movement, while now there is the keenest emulation in heaping up the highest honors on those who have succeeded in this fight to make New York not only greater, but better; now there is very little anonymous sympathy.

Another cause of the awakening which should have a large place is the legal proof of the existence of the corruption in our city administration. For that reason we owe a debt of gratitude to the Investigating Committee. It is a very easy matter to bring accusations of malfeasance in office and charges of corruption in a municipal department, but it is a very difficult matter to prove such allegations. The community now has *legal* proof of what before was only *moral* certainty of the existing corruption. We were all pretty sure that the police were venal, that vice was protected and virtue defenseless, that there was a criminal collusion between the criminal classes and those who should have been their sworn enemies; but how many of us would have gone into court with our

* *The New York Herald*, November 7, 1894.

moral certitude of the prevalent wrong-doing? and even if we had, what would have been the legal worth of such opinions? The lack of legal proof is the rock on which so many so-called reformers suffer shipwreck. The fact that Dr. Parkhurst has only made charges that he can defend with a whole battery of facts has made him the dread of all the evil-doers in the city, and has given him a scourge with which he can lash them relentlessly.

The insistence that was laid on non-partizanship, not only in New York, but in other cities, was a large element of the success of the last election. And the result of the election has not lessened the need. From a study of nearly all the municipal reform movements in the United States the great majority consider non-partizanship of prime importance. Measures, not men, must take the place of the party cries; and, unless it is taken for granted, the qualifying adjective "good" must precede "measures." No one party can claim that it alone was responsible for the overturning of civic misrule in New York, and no one party could have made it possible. In matters affecting the welfare of a great municipality questions of party have no place and should not be tolerated. Our civic servants should be selected with the same disregard of their party affiliations that you use when you select a clerk, a butler, or a coachman. Who ever heard of a Republican park or playground, a Democratic swimming-bath, a Prohibition street-cleaning department, or a Populist mortuary? In federal politics let us cling as tenaciously as we please to the strictest party lines, but in municipal politics there can be no party lines. Professor James Bryce clearly grasped this principle when he recently wrote me: "It has always seemed to me that among the things most needed in American municipal life are, first, less intrusion of party feeling into the city elections. . . ." Non-partizanship in the coming months is an element which must not be disregarded by all true reformers.

Hatred of bosses was another factor in the rescue of the city from misrule. As Dr. Strong so clearly demonstrated at the opening Municipal Program Conference, the great struggle of 1861–65 * was fought because the principle of federation was imperiled; but by the conclusion of the war that question was settled. Then the soldier and the sailor, and the men who had upheld the Union with their money and their influence, turned their attention to the restoration of their business concerns and the extension of their private affairs. They were too much absorbed in them to pay attention to the management of the city—that might look out for itself. Then came the practical politician, the man who had the time and was willing to give his best thought to the care of the municipality. He was willing to such an extent that in some cases he paid $2000 election expenses for an office of which the salary was $1500. These are the men who, as one of their own number stated it, are not in politics for their health. To throw sand in your eyes these same practical politicians took the utmost pains to put the tax-rate at the lowest notch, but at the same time doubled the valuation of the taxable property. They kept Fifth Avenue scrupulously clean, and made Central Park the peer of any in the world; but while doing all this to lull your suspicions, their henchmen made the ignorant Hebrews on the East Side pay two dollars for the privilege of voting, and annual legislation appropriating money for a park in Mulberry Bend afforded a choice playground for these same men. The voice of the people at the last election expressed itself against the bosses. One king-boss heard the muttering of the elements and, like a prudent man, withdrew before the storm

* Note the rapid growth of the before unimportant cities after this period. We are now a nation of cities.

broke; another remains, persisting in thinking that his occupation is not yet gone, but if he continues to obstruct the popular will, he will learn that political cyclones move in circles. A recent utterance of Dr. Parkhurst on the boss has great weight:

"You must remember that there is a big difference between a leader and a boss. The leader is he who has the power of reproducing his own conceptions, his own ideas, in the minds of those who are in any way subjected to his interests. The office of the leader is to make more and more of the man in any way brought under his impress. The object of the boss is to make less and less of the man who is brought in any way under him. The boss is the most sagaciously devised scheme ever originated for the purpose of crushing out, weakening, and drying up in the individual all manly personality. And this is why we pledge ourselves to fight the boss, whatever may be his province and whatever may be his pretensions to respectability. The more respectable he is the more damnably dangerous he is."*

The fact that the victory for reform was won in New York is of great importance. The position of this city is strategic, not only for the State, but for the entire country. In addition, the eyes of the entire world were upon us, for it was well known that we were suffering from the very worst government that has yet fallen upon any of our cities. Republican institutions were on trial, and outside cities and nations wondered if we could shake off the despotism of misrule. When, therefore, we did rise in our civic might, and said, "Thus far and no farther," the friends of good government all over the country took fresh courage, and said to themselves, "If New York can free herself we can." That is the reason that the victory in our city has so much significance. Emphasizing this statement, at the formal opening of the Teachers' Col-

* *The City Vigilant*, December, 1894.

lege, President Gilman, of the Johns Hopkins University, remarked:

"New York is an example to all this land—a colossal object-lesson. It is in itself a sort of teachers' college where other cities may learn both what to do and what not to do. It suffers a bad municipal organization for years, then overturns it in a day with the battery of the ten commandments. Other cities may follow or neglect the lessons, but are sure to watch, weigh, and judge what happens on the island of Manhattan. The Central Park is opened—similar parks appear in Boston and San Francisco; museums devoted to the works of nature and art are established—Washington and Chicago begin the like; Columbia unites the institutions of higher education in a federative union—Baltimore longs to do the same. Here and now the unfolding of a new idea is celebrated—an idea not absolutely new, but new in its environment and possibilities. The leaders of education in other cities, in surprise and delight, will note, praise, emulate the suggestions here embodied, the generosity with which they have been supported, the enthusiasm which has governed their development."

How shall the victory be utilized to the utmost? In the first place, there should be a Municipal Council for the Greater New York. If the Municipal Program Conferences* have any one hobby it is the need of what is positive in our municipal program. Now that we have made ourselves obnoxious by our insistence on that principle, and have done our best to introduce that idea among the community, we will proceed to the next step; but do not then think that you have heard the

---

* "Found: A Municipal Program. The Greater and Better New York. A Series of Conferences of those interested in Good Municipal Government, held in the Amity Building, 312 West 54th Street, under the Auspices of the Nineteenth Assembly District of the City Vigilance League, on Alternate Thursday Evenings, at Eight O'clock, during the season of 1894-5."

last of the hobby. The consensus of opinion among the promoters of these conferences is that the next step must be the appointment of a Municipal Council. The work done by the Committee of Seventy was necessary and of the greatest value; but that organization was not a representative body, in that it was not chosen by the city; it therefore had no official sanction. Now there should be such a committee, board, or council, but it should have permanent and official recognition. This sanction should result from the popular election of its membership. As James C. Carter so truly said at a public dinner, "The overthrow of the last election was volcanic, and will not occur again this generation." The practical politicians know this, and at this very minute are laying their plans for the old line of action, just as soon as the public shall have gone to sleep again. Civic insomnia is a disease for which these physicians seldom prescribe. The limits of this chapter will not permit the description of the organization or the duties of such a council, but the pressing need at the present time is for some machine, steady, constant, and untiring, that shall be the instrument for the transmission of an enlightened public opinion. Now, if you also believe it, give currency to the idea; discuss the need and its solution among your friends; then some day you will learn of its realization, and you will have been responsible to a certain extent for its creation. That will be practical politics.

The work of destruction has been successful, and the dust from the crash of the overthrown walls of the hall is slowly disappearing. The era ahead is therefore one of upbuilding, constructive, positive. Leighton Williams very wisely pressed the need of the educational phases of reform work, because misrule is largely made possible through the ignorance of citizens. Your indifference to matters of civic import is one element in the continuance of political ignorance. Accordingly every ounce of social and political education will yield tons of good citizenship. It is your duty, therefore, to encourage, just as much as in you lies, whatever will promote the civic education of your fellows. That is why Vigilance Leagues, Good Government Clubs, and conferences are of great value. They secure attention and then stimulate it by giving their members something to do. Illustrating this point from the constitution of the City Vigilance League:

"The objects of this League shall be to quicken among its members an appreciation of their municipal obligations; to acquaint them with existing conditions; to familiarize them with the machinery of municipal government; to make conspicuous the respects in which such government is languidly or criminally administered; to regard with jealous concern the point at which private interest enters into competition with the general good; and in every possible way to repress in the community what makes for its detriment, and to foster whatsoever seems fitted to promote its advantage."

The people must be trusted, and in so far as they are deprived of a share in civic affairs, to that extent have they suffered. If we are a republic and a democracy we must return to that principle, from which we have been straying far afield in the last few years. But while the above facts are true, it is also true, in my opinion, that the masses do not lead in any great reform. When the leader arises they give or withhold their support, and the movement in question succeeds or fails. Men crave leaders, and instinctively look up to those who will guide them under the inspiration of a great cause; hence we have a Savonarola, a Luther, and a Parkhurst. It is that fact which justifies the remarks of Dr. Albert Shaw concerning the latter reformer:

"And it should further be borne in mind that this unprecedented revolution in the public sentiment of New York City has come about as a direct consequence of the untiring and persistent attacks of the Rev. Charles H. Parkhurst, D.D., upon the one point of the criminal corruption of the police department. A great lesson has thus been taught to reformers everywhere. Dr. Parkhurst has shown what can be accomplished by intrepidity and by everlasting persistence. He began his work with little public favor. Even the ministers of the various denominations of New York came to his support in scant numbers. Hundreds of them either publicly or privately expressed disapproval of his methods. But Dr. Parkhurst never flinched for a moment, although he must have suffered keenly from the slanders of his enemies and the distrust of those who ought to have been his friends. But everything is different now. Dr. Parkhurst is the most authoritative citizen of New York. No one dares to speak of him with disrespect. He continues to denounce Tammany with an intensity that no one else can equal; yet even Tammany is at length subdued and deferential in its attitude toward Dr. Parkhurst. And all the newspapers are his humble and obedient servants. Nothing like this personal victory has ever been witnessed, so far as we are aware, in any American community. Yet not for a moment at any point has Dr. Parkhurst shown himself unequal to this new and still more difficult *rôle* of unquestioned primacy and authority. He maintains the same attitude of disinterestedness and self-forgetfulness."*

The leader, therefore, is useless without the following of the masses, and *vice versa.* Just as in the industrial world there can be no divided interests between labor and capital, so in municipal affairs leaders and the people are essential. How is the attention of the people to be gained? When the Tweed ring was smashed, and, in our own day, when the Wigwam was made desolate, it was the disclosure of the corruption incident to each *régime* that held the public attention. Truly a strange situation when corruption is necessary to rivet the public gaze and hold the public ear! The 6th of November clearly proved that the awakened public opinion would be no longer outraged,

* *Review of Reviews,* November, 1894.

and a halt has been called. Which is better: that we shall suffer a relapse, until attention can only be aroused by the uncovering of sores and the removal of cancers from the body politic, or that the civic mind shall be kept active and stimulated by a policy that will make it healthful and hardy?

The prophetic office is not always a sinecure. I consider that I should be remiss in my duty unless I should point out certain manifest dangers. In the present situation there are discordant elements. Unless these can be overcome and harmonized so that the rallying-cry shall be civic righteousness and non-partizanship the victory will not be permanent. If it be always true that history repeats itself it will be of advantage for a moment to take a backward glance, but with the determination of guarding against the repetition of the evil. I quote from a paper prepared by Miss Putnam:

"In 1821 a bill was passed in the legislature providing for the submission to the people at the spring election of the question of a constitutional convention. That election was important for New York, and the *Evening Post*, then in its twentieth year, published repeated appeals to the voters to come out and cast their ballots. The election took place the third week in April, and the returns came in slowly. Saturday, April 28th, the *Post* announced that the last reports, as brought in by steamboat, justified a rejoicing over the result: 'This will convince the demagogues of Tammany Hall that their influence has received its death-blow, and that we are not to depend on the breath of their nostrils. Men will be distinguished and rewarded according to their merits, and not according to the dictates of a Jacobin club. Their time is come; they are fallen, never to rise on their grizzly heads again.' The *Post* then thought that it was not too soon to triumph over Tammany's downfall, and that was seventy-three years ago." *

* "The Extension of the Franchise: What Constitutes a State Voter" (Miss Ruth Putnam).

A great victory has been won, but the general well knows that a victory does not end the campaign. The routed enemy must be followed up, in order to prevent him from making a second stand; his camp must be destroyed and his base of supplies cut off. A very pertinent question arises: "What are we going to do about it?" What encouragement that the community will not again hibernate? I claim with confidence that there are many reasons why I am particularly hopeful that this great victory will not be lost. The chief source of encouragement lies in the fact that there are so many organized movements in the churches, particularly for the young people. The waves of organizing fervor are now subsiding, and the spirit of spiritual self-complacency has already exerted a deleterious influence, so that the leaders are very wisely affording fresh fuel for the flaming desire of doing something. In my opinion, unless this had been done very soon, these great societies would have burned themselves out. The fresh fuel that is being heaped on the dying fires is an interest in good citizenship, in which the pioneers are the Y. P. S. C. E. Quoting from one of these movements in Omaha: "The purpose of this League shall be the education of the Christian people of Omaha in the conditions and needs of our city, and their duties as citizens to its municipal government." This is the kind of standard needed, and when the other societies attain it we shall have an enlightened body of young men and women who will make a stand for their rights as citizens, inasmuch as they know what they are; and because they are Christian citizens they will be just as ready to fulfil their duties.

The victorious results will be far more permanent if we will only take a more hopeful view of the situation. I am fully aware of the dangers of an excessive optimism, but taken in moderate doses it will be efficacious. Why should we not use what we have gained as a vantage-ground for the next upward step? The vaulted roof of the cathedral does not spring from the columns till the foundations have been laid deep and sure. The ground has now been cleared of obstructions and leveled for the foundation of our civic temple, and it will be your fault if the walls do not begin to rise. We should not be despondent because the carvings of the pillars, the fretwork of the ceiling, and the splendor of the spire may not form an harmonious whole; our immediate business is with the foundation. After striking the balance the present municipal situation is encouraging, and would be still more so were it not for the pessimistic croakers, who are almost as bad as the boss Crokers. I therefore maintain that every one who is distrustful that the reform will not be permanent, that the old conditions of misrule will very soon return, who begins all his sentences with an "if"— such persons are blocking the reform movement, and to the extent that they express such sentiments are retarding the progress of events.

In order that this reform movement may be utilized to the utmost the material and commercial spirit in our civic life must be subordinated to the progressive and social spirit of the times, because this new social spirit will not be satisfied with a municipal policy that will content itself with a low tax-rate and a successful policing of the city; it will absolutely condemn the heartless and commercial greed of a sugar or of any other great trust that will close its works, throwing hundreds of employees out of work. Many of the so-called reform movements have yet to learn this lesson, that commercial and material prosperity are not the sole foundations of the true welfare of a city. Do not misunderstand me. I do not say that they are valueless, but they are only means to an end, and that end is a city which shall be a home for all the component parts. To illustrate concretely what I have been saying, I quote from the constitution of a reform organization: "We believe the accomplishment of the above purpose will promote the material growth and advance the commercial interests of this city, and to this end we invite the coöperation of all our fellow-citizens." New York is one of the richest cities in the world, while the evidences of material and commercial splendor abound on every side, unless, perchance, you are on the East Side. Tell me of what advantage now, at this very minute, is this wealth to the wage-earners, who may wish to improve their condition by attendance at a technical or a manual-training school, who may be desirous of visiting a public library, who would enjoy the recreation of an art gallery or a museum, or who would gratify any of the desires that you consider so essential to your happiness? It is no answer to the question for you to say that they will not appreciate such advantages, because you have never given them a chance. I would therefore beg of you not to be drawn too far away from the problems of pressing interest by a consideration of voting-machines, the blanket ballot, honest primaries, and the sale of the salt-works, but to use your efforts in the enforcement of the positive program, because that will at once conduce to the true welfare of what should be your city.

II

MUNICIPAL REFORM MOVEMENTS

I am strongly impressed with the belief that municipal reform proceeds haltingly in the United States because, for one reason, many citizens who desire sincerely to aid in the regeneration of their town life and neighborhood affairs have formed no definite municipal ideals. They have neither learned what in the experience of the world has come to be regarded as a sound constitution or framework of municipal government, nor have they made up their minds to what positive tasks and public services a municipal government may wisely apply itself. . . . City government in America defeats its own ends by its " checks and balances," its partitions of duty and responsibility, and its grand opportunities for hide-and-seek. . . . Cheerful and rational acceptance of urban life as a great social fact demands that the city government should proceed to make such urban life conduce positively to the welfare of all the people whose lawful interests bring them together as denizens of great towns.

ALBERT SHAW.

II

MUNICIPAL REFORM MOVEMENTS

THE ADVANCE CLUB

President,　　　　　　　　　*Secretary,*
HIRAM HOWARD.　　　　　SAMUEL W. KILVERT,
　　　　　　　　　　　　　　Providence, R. I.

THIS Club was incorporated in 1892. According to its constitution the Club was organized to promote the business and material interests of the city of Providence, to cultivate a broad and liberal public spirit among its citizens, and to assist in the course of education, particularly in the lines of industrial pursuits.

The Club purposes, among other things, to devote itself to the work of encouraging new business enterprises in its city, of extending its foreign and domestic trade, and of promoting public improvements and sanitary measures.

The executive committee consists of fifteen members, with the following departments of work:

1. Entertainment.
2. Publication.
3. Promotion of Manufactures and Trade.
4. Water, Sewerage, and Sanitary Conditions.
5. Education.
6. Parks and Public Buildings.
7. Railroads and Transportation.

8. Marine Commerce and Harbor Improvements.
9. Highways.
10. Municipal Reform.

The initiation fee is $10, and the annual dues $25.

AMERICAN INSTITUTE OF CIVICS

President,
HENRY RANDALL WAITE, PH.D.

Secretary,
HON. W. E. SHELDON,
3 Somerset Street,
Boston, Mass.

The Institute was organized in 1885 and incorporated under the laws of Congress in 1887. There are no salaried offices. The object, as stated in the constitution, is to promote good government and right social order by elevating the standard of citizenship. There are three classes of members—life, honorary, and active. An executive committee of eleven meets at the call of the chairman. There are no salaried officials in the Institute. The work is directed by means of seven departments:

1. Extension.
2. Department of Public-school Work.
3. Business-school Department.
4. College and Professional-school Department.
5. Press Department.
6. Department of Salutary Legislation.
7. Department of Applied Ethics.

The organ of the Institute is a monthly, the *American Magazine of Civics*. By this means, and through its staff of officers and lecturers, to the number of five hundred and twenty, in all parts of the country, the organization comes in touch with its members. The local branches are known as clubs and councils, which exist in several of the larger cities. The

Institute is strictly non-partizan. Women are eligible. The Institute calls to its membership only those who are willing to aid in its advancement; but the character and the extent of this aid is intended to be chiefly a matter of individual judgment, according to personal and local conditions and opportunities. Members as individuals, or in connection with local councils, at the cost of little effort, have rendered such aid. They have done this by interesting popular organizations in the discussion of citizenship duties; by lectures, or provision for lectures (free, if possible), before lyceums, working-men's clubs, young people's associations, and other suitable organizations, secular and religious; by securing the salutary observance of patriotic anniversaries; by promoting adequate instruction in civics in all schools; by coöperation in efforts to secure the wise and honest administration of public affairs; by promoting the local and State legislation and other action necessary to the purity of the ballot, honesty and efficiency in the civil service, the integrity and highest usefulness of the public schools, the maintenance of law and order, and the promotion of social purity.

ANTI-SPOILS LEAGUE

President,
CARL SCHURZ.

Secretary,
GEORGE MCANENY,
54 William Street,
New York.

The League was organized in 1893, in affiliation with the National Civil-service Reform League, and having for its officers the officers of that organization. Its object is the complete abolition of the spoils system from the public service. It secures financial support from voluntary contributors. The members are called "subscribing"—that is, those who subscribe their names to the League's declaration:

"We hereby declare ourselves in favor of the complete abolition of the spoils system from the public service, believing that system to be unjust, undemocratic, injurious to political parties, fruitful of corruption, a burden to legislative and executive officers, and in every way opposed to the principles of good government.

"We call upon all in authority to extend to the utmost the operation of the present reform laws, and by additional legislation to carry the benefits of the merit system to the farthest practicable limits under our national, State, and municipal governments."

The League was formed under the auspices of the National Civil-service Reform League, upon the suggestion of Mr. Richard Watson Gilder. Its purpose was to bring together in a compact body those who are willing to affirm their opposition to the spoils system in national, State, or municipal government, and to aid, as their opportunities may allow, in the efforts making toward its eradication. Among the results already accomplished have been the general dissemination of information regarding the civil-service reform movement, and the promotion of various local movements for municipal and other reforms. The League now has upon its rolls the names of about ten thousand members, located in almost every State and Territory.

THE CITIZENS' ASSOCIATION OF ALBANY

President,
J. HOWARD KING.

Secretary,
DAVID A. THOMPSON,
Albany, N. Y.

The Citizens' Association of Albany was organized in January, 1881. The Board of Supervisors of that county had not then finally adjourned, although most of the county accounts had been audited.

It was about this time reported that gross frauds had been perpetrated upon the county by the presentation of fictitious claims by certain coroners and undertakers; and the Association, on inquiry, found that only three or four years before similar frauds had been discovered, but that public attention had not been called to the fact, and the guilty parties had not been prosecuted.

The Association seeks to promote the interests of neither political party, but expects to convince both parties that when dishonest and corrupt men are nominated for office citizens will have the independence not to vote for them, and to warn those who seek office simply for the purpose of plundering the public treasury that their malfeasance in office will be exposed; and, if that be not a sufficient argument, that criminal proceedings will be taken against them.

Its paid attorney, J. Fenimore Cooper, Esq., scans all claims presented on verified forms to the county Board of Supervisors, or Common Council, and enjoins the payment of such as are illegal or unauthorized. The executive committee has done much good by introducing new and defeating bad legislation affecting the city and county. The Committee of Thirteen directs the work of the Association. Each member of the Association who is taxed in the county of Albany for real or personal property, or both, to the amount of $25,000 or more, pays an annual fee of $25. If a member is assessed between $10,000 and $25,000, his fee is $10, and $5 when the assessment is less than $10,000.

The committee makes this statement in its last report:

"The committee has been thus far enabled to pursue a course unfettered by entangling alliances, and uninfluenced by personal interests or political prejudices or predilections.

"It has attempted to represent and protect an element in our municipal commonwealth which finds but slight recognition in a political government where most (with a few honorable exceptions) of those who control our public affairs 'are so busied in their private concernments that they have neither leisure to study the public interest nor are safely to be trusted with it, because a man is not faithfully embarked in this kind of a ship if he has no share in the freight.'

"It has prepared and procured the passage, from year to year, of many statutes which have regulated and reorganized our local administration.

"It has secured judicial decisions preventing and punishing the pillage of the public treasury.

"Above all, it has sought to mold public sentiment from chaotic clamor into well-defined purposes of redress, and to open paths of remedy for public wrongs. For in the purpose and pathway of public opinion lie the preëminent elements of its past success and all the possibilities of its future."

CITIZENS' ASSOCIATION OF BOSTON

President,
CAUSTEN BROWNE.

Secretary,
HERBERT L. HARDING,
89 State Street,
Boston, Mass.

December 27, 1887, was the date of organization, but the Association is unincorporated. The secretary occupies a salaried position, as he acts as counsel to the Association. The society is supported by subscriptions and annual assessments of $10 on the members. According to the constitution:

"The purpose of the Association shall be to promote an honest, efficient, and economical administration of municipal and county affairs, by inducing the citizens and taxpayers to take a more active and intelligent interest in such affairs, by furnishing an accurate and non-partizan account of the manner in which the city is governed and of the conduct of the public servants, by encouraging faithful and exposing unfaithful performance of official duties, and by advocating legislation necessary or proper for securing its purpose.

"It shall be the endeavor of the Association to keep a careful watch over the expenditures of public money, the making and performance of contracts, the purchase of supplies and material, and the passage of measures by the City Council; to prevent illegal, fraudulent, or improper payments from the city or county treasury; to investigate alleged official misconduct, to bring to punishment all who may be parties to such misconduct, and to ascertain and report any facts which, in the interest of good government, should be known by the citizens of Boston."

Thirteen comprise the executive committee, who meet twice a month and assign the work to the following departments:

1. Finance.
2. Law.
3. Membership.
4. General Committee (thirty members).

The Association does not take partizan action in advancing the nomination or election of candidates for public office; but in carrying out the purpose of the Association, as set forth above, it may publish information relating to such candidates, and may oppose the eleetion of any candidate whose defeat may appear to be demanded in the public interest. There is no organ of the Association. Women are eligible to membership. In answer to the inquiry, What are the results actually accomplished by the Association? the secretary writes:

"It is rather difficult for me to place any correct estimate upon the relative value of our various efforts. We have accomplished, unquestionably, a great deal of good, both directly and indirectly; that is to say, we have affirmatively accomplished many good results, or we have prevented, by our timely and effective opposition, many injurious consequences by direct action; and we have also indirectly accomplished other work of perhaps larger value by awakening the public conscience, calling attention to needed reforms, and showing the citizens what they ought to have and how they can get it. For instance, we have prevented by our effective opposition various attempts to raise the debt and tax limitations now imposed by statute; we have prevented by interference and exposure many fraudulent and improper proceedings, like the purchase of land, the payment of large sums of money in settlement of disputed claims, the improper settlement of suits brought against boodlers, and other things of this sort. We have undoubtedly been the means of defeating one or two objectionable measures which would otherwise have been passed by the legislature, in regard to franchises in our streets and alleged rapid-transit measures. We were the means, four years ago, of exposing to public ridicule and contempt a most unworthy candidate for the mayoralty, who challenged us in regard to his character. The exposure which we were forced to make of him, followed by his ignominious attempts at explanation, resulted in delivering the city from the control of a most corrupt man, as he has since proved to be, for he fled the town.

"As a sample of the indirect good which has resulted from our work, I might mention lower rates for electric-light service, the removal and burying of overhead wires, the reorganization of certain executive departments of the city government upon business principles, the defeat and the passage of many measures by the State legislature and City Council."

THE CITIZENS' ASSOCIATION

President,
JOHN C. GRAVES.

Treasurer,
H. C. HARROWER,
Buffalo, N. Y.

The organization of the Association was effected in 1888, but there is no permanent secretary. The Committee on Legislation is practically an executive committee, and consists of nine members, meeting at the call of the chairman. There is also a Committee on Separate Local Elections. There is no membership of women, although there is nothing to prevent their taking part in the work of the Association. The original object of the society was the reform of the city charter, but since 1891, when the revised charter was adopted, its work has been to protect and improve it. Other matters of local and general interest in municipal affairs are discussed.

The Citizens' Association is a wholly indefinite body. It has no membership, properly speaking, no constitution, and no by-laws. Its first active members, who framed the revised charter and carried it through, were chiefly delegates sent from all the other organized bodies of citizens—of the various professions, trades, and commercial bodies, local associations, etc. But even this skeleton organization has now been abandoned. The president, who is practically a permanent officer, calls public meetings on the floor of the Merchants' Exchange whenever there is a demand for action. Any one is at liberty to attend, to speak, and to vote. They are practically town-meetings, though the attendance is usually not large. The local press gladly gives publicity to such meetings, and the action taken commands such authority as responsive public sentiment gives it. A few standing committees have charge of matters upon which the Association has formulated opinions in the past. One of these, the Committee on Legislation, is expected to watch all proposed charter amendments. Another, the Committee on Separate Local Elections, has been instructed by repeated resolutions to take action to promote some general scheme for the entire separation, in point of time, of all the local elections in cities and large counties from State and national elections.

THE CITIZENS' ASSOCIATION OF CHICAGO

President,
I. K. BOYESEN.

Secretary,
J. C. AMBLER,
33 Merchants' Building,
Chicago, Ill.

The Association was organized July 24, 1874, but has not been incorporated. The secretary holds a salaried position. The preamble of the Association's constitution states:

"In order to insure a more perfect administration in our municipal affairs; to promote the general welfare and prosperity of the city; to protect citizens, so far as possible, against the evils of careless or corrupt legislation; to effect the prompt enforcement and execution of the law; to foster and encourage all enterprises necessary and calculated to develop and extend our business and commercial interests; to protect and maintain our credit, both at home and abroad; to secure such legislation, both State and national, as the interests of the city may from time to time require; to arouse a more widely extended interest in our municipal legislation and administration; to correct existing abuses, and to prevent their future recurrence; and believing that, to secure these ends, organized and united action is necessary;

"We, citizens, taxpayers, and voters, in the city of Chicago, have formed this Association, and for its government have established this constitution.

"The general purposes of this Association shall be those set forth in the preamble to this constitution, employing such means to execute those purposes as this Association may from time to time adopt."

Financial support is obtained from the membership fees. An executive committee of fifteen meets each week. This committee appoints standing committees:

1. Advisory.
2. Finance.
3. City and County Administration.
4. State Legislation.
5. Taxation.

The Association does not take any active part in politics. Women are eligible to membership, but none have yet joined. As there is no organ of the society, it comes in touch with the workers by means of the executive committee. As to results actually accomplished, the executive committee has compiled in chronological form the principal transactions of the Association since its organization. This was the record for 1892–93:

Legislation.—Promoting projects for the reform of our *city and county administration* by efforts to obtain a constitutional convention. Favoring the bill for *registration of land-titles* on the Australian plan. The peculiarity of the political situation prevented, as in 1883, any beneficial legislation except of a general character.

Police Courts.—Continuing the investigation begun last year, and with marked success, as cannot be denied upon comparison of the two periods.

Keeping the public advised at all times of attempts to infringe their rights, and either by publication or otherwise calling attention to public grievances and suggesting remedies.

Attending to the general interests of the city by observations and action with regard to main and house drainage, stenches, smoke, whistles, both marine and stationary, street obstructions, fast driving, pavements, water-supply, sanitation, usurious loans to poor people, and other business which has become *regular.*

CITIZENS' CLUB

President,
JULIUS DEXTER.

Secretary,
NATHANIEL HENCHMAN DAVIS,
64 West Third Street,
Cincinnati, O.

This Club, organized in 1893, is the successor of the Committee of One Hundred, organized in October, 1885. The secretary at present holds a salaried position.

The Citizens' Club has been organized to promote honest and efficient administration of local affairs. The objects of the Club will be sought through its officers and executive committee, principally by *insistence* that public officials shall keep within their duties, especially in the expenditure of public money, and shall wholly comply with the requirements of law.

Statutes of doubtful legality will be contested, especially when they involve debt or taxation. Generally criticism will be applied to city and county affairs, and as far as possible correct and accurate information will be collected and published about local administration.

In brief, it will be the duty of the Club to call attention to such abuses of power as require correction, and to apply the remedies provided by law.

The Club will try to supply the place mentioned in the old saying, "What is everybody's business is nobody's business;" and as vigilance is the price of immunity from official abuse, this organization will, if properly sustained by sufficient financial means and the moral support of this community, be vigilant and aggressive for the public good.

The annual membership fee is $5. The executive committee of nine meets at the call of the chair. The Club is restricted in its political action. Women are ineligible to membership.

The Committee of One Hundred was organized in October, 1885, to purify the city and county government, and correct abuses in the administration of the elections and the police department, all of which were in a very scandalous condition. The Committee prosecuted and succeeded in sending to the State penitentiary eight or ten men, some of them *prominent* officers of the city government, for fraud either in the administration of the government or in the elections. The Committee succeeded in having passed by the legislature the Election Bill, establishing registration of voters, and reserving one hundred feet each side of the polling-places; the nonpartizan board of four members then created is still in existence, and gives general satisfaction. It also had the Police Bill passed, establishing a non(bi)-partizan board, which is still in existence; and though it has not always been as satisfactory as the Election Board, has finally given the city one of the very best police forces in this country, as it now requires both a mental and a very careful physical examination of all applicants.

The Citizens' Club pays especial attention to the letting of contracts and the levying of taxes.

THE CITIZENS' FEDERATION OF TOLEDO

Secretary,
E. P. MULL,
113 Superior Street,
Toledo, O.

October 10, 1894, the organization was effected, under a voluntary secretary, but the entire board of officers has not yet been chosen. The respective chairmen of the Pastors' Union and the Christian Endeavor County Union organized the Federation. Some of the strongest business men and lawyers in the city are enlisted, with the support of their money and service, as far as they can possibly devote it. There is an advisory board, made up of a representative from each denomination and religious society in the city. The object of the society, as stated in its constitution, is to promote good citizenship; to assist in the enforcement of national, State, and municipal laws; to encourage and insist on the maintenance of good government. The executive committee of seven meets once a week. There are four departments of work:

1. Gambling.
2. Saloons.
3. Sunday Desecrations.
4. Disorderly Houses.

The ward is the lowest unit of organization, and the society is unrestricted in its political action. Women are eligible to membership. The recent organization has not admitted of any results actually accomplished.

CITIZENS' LEAGUE

President,
LUTHER H. KELLAM.

Secretary,
HENRY HOLLINGSHED, JR.,
111 Market Street,
Camden, N. J.

The society, under its present name, was organized October, 1893, but is not incorporated. The League seemed to have grown out of a variety of causes, the principal of which was the controlling influence which the Gloucester race-track and kindred vicious powers exerted upon both political parties, dictating nominations, controlling election boards, "fixing" up the count, and generally manipulating the elections so that in no event would the friends of law and order get any control. In addition the courts were tampered with, juries fixed, the race-track owners and *habitués* protected at all hazard or at any cost. A voluntary secretary has charge of the work, and voluntary contributions furnish financial support. During the campaign a newspaper called the *Citizens' League* is published. The objects of the League, as stated in its platform, are:

"1. We demand the election of city and county officials upon a strictly non-partizan basis, integrity and fitness being the only qualities required.

"2. We demand the reduction of the present high taxes, as far as is consistent with the proper conduct of public affairs, and a just and proper return of benefits to the people for all the burdens of taxation.

"3. We denounce the present useless multiplication of offices, and we demand from our legislature the repeal of all laws which deprive our citizens of the right of self-government, and especially those which tend to destroy temperance and morality."

The leading result of these demands has been better nominations by the dominant party. Women are ineligible to membership.

CITIZENS' LEAGUE OF NEW ROCHELLE

President,
JOHN O. OFFORD.

Secretary,
W. B. GREELY,
39 Leland Avenue,
New Rochelle, N. Y.

This League was organized February 22, 1894, with a voluntary secretary. The association was effected from the desire of the citizens to free themselves from ring rule. As stated in its constitution, "its object shall be the securing of good government in town and village on non-partizan lines." The executive committee of nine meets at the call of the president. There is as yet but one department of work, namely, on organization, which works within each election district. There is no constitutional provision excluding women from membership, but there are none at present. Voluntary contributions support the League, and it is not restricted in political action. Membership in the League may be obtained, on application to the chairman of the proper sub-committee on organization, by any one believing in non-partizan local government, to be confirmed by signing the roll of members of his district.

The Citizens' League of New Rochelle is a strictly non-partizan organization, and its sole object is to promote honest, faithful, and economical government in town and village affairs. To this end its aim is to secure by all lawful means the election of competent, intelligent, and reliable men, whose character will not only be an assurance of their conscientious discharge of duty, but also of the correction of existing abuses.

The policy of the League is either the indorsement of eligible candidates nominated by any of the political parties, or, in default of such nominations, the selection of independent candidates who may be commended with confidence to the suffrages of the people.

In noting the results actually accomplished it has been learned that in the village election held April 17, 1894, the influence of the League was instrumental in securing the election of one trustee against the ring candidate, and in reducing the expected majorities of the other ring candidates—in one case to two and in another to less than ten. In the recent school-board election the ring candidates were defeated by an overwhelming majority—a result due largely to the work of the League in the village election.

THE CITIZENS' LEAGUE OF THE TOWN OF NORWALK

Secretary,
CHARLES HELMER, JR.,
20 West Street,
South Norwalk, Conn.

The saloons were becoming unbearable, and corrupting politics and officials increasing alarmingly, when a meeting was called June, 1894, to form an Anti-Saloon League. At the meeting it was voted to make it broader, and the name Citizens' League was adopted. The growth has been rapid. Men of all parties, creeds, and beliefs are coming in. Membership now numbers about one hundred and fifty—all strong, influential men. The chief object is against the saloon, because it is believed to be the center of vice, crime, and corruption in politics. Hence the aim is at the saloon, but at the same time other things are not forgotten. According to its constitution, "the object of the League shall be the consolidation and increase of anti-liquor-saloon sentiment; the education of citizens as to the nature of the licensed saloon; the increase of the no-license vote; the suppression of saloons and *all social evils* in every legitimate way; and the stimulating of interest in the performance of the *civic duties*."

The membership fee is $1 a year. The present temporary executive committee is composed of seven members, meeting at the call of the president. Standing committees have been appointed on:

1. Finance.
2. Membership.
3. Educational Meetings.
4. Educational Literature.
5. Elections.
6. Law and Order.
7. Saloon Licenses.

The League is not restricted in its political action. Women are ineligible to membership. The League is of too recent an origin to have a long list of things actually accomplished, but it has aroused a deep public sentiment, resulting in the nomination and election of good officers and the better enforcement of existing laws.

CITIZENS' MUNICIPAL ASSOCIATION OF PHILADELPHIA

President,
JOEL J. BAILY.

Secretary,
GEORGE BURNHAM, JR.,
1213 Filbert Street,
Philadelphia, Pa.

The society was organized April 20, 1886, and incorporated April 30, 1887. The secretary holds a voluntary position, but the Association employs an agent who receives a salary and is allowed a stenographer. Annual dues from members and voluntary contributions support the organization. The executive committee consists of twenty-one, who meet regularly once a month. The departments of work are five:

1. Finance.
2. Membership.
3. Abuses and Complaints.
4. Law and Legislation.
5. Room and Library.

According to its constitution the objects of the Association shall be:

"1. To sustain the constituted authorities in a faithful administration of the public service.

"2. To secure a strict fulfilment by public officers, employees, and contractors of all their obligations to the city and to the citizen.

"3. To promote such legislation as shall be most conducive to the public welfare."

The Association has no organ, but is generally sustained by the newspapers in Philadelphia, which freely publish its communications and transactions when desired. Not taking any political action, the Association does not come in contact with the workers, if by this term political workers are meant. If the term refers to workers in the Association, all the work is done by the agent and the members of the executive committee. There are no district organizations. Political action is restricted, in that the Association shall take no part in nominations or elections to public office. While there are no women members, there is nothing in the constitution of the Association rendering them ineligible. Among the results actually accomplished the secretary writes:

"Stricter compliance with contracts generally; litigation to determine liability of street-car companies to pave streets occupied by them with 'improved pavement,' largely forwarded by efforts of this Association; decision of Supreme Court favorable to city finally obtained, resulting in recovery of several hundred thousand dollars from companies, and many miles of improved pavements; recently expert report on asphalt pavement caused opening of bids to free competition and saving of fifty cents per yard on all pavements laid this year—this examination and report undertaken in connection with the Trades League of this city. There are many other matters which have been considered by our Association, too numerous to mention, in which hundreds of thousands of dollars have been saved to the taxpayers of Philadelphia."

This Association was the outgrowth of the Committee of One Hundred, a reform political organization, disbanded January 19, 1886. It was determined to pursue the work in which said committee had been successful, viz., the non-political work.

THE CITIZENS' MUNICIPAL LEAGUE

President,
CLEMENT W. SHOEMAKER.

Secretary,
EDWARD M. FITHIAN,
Bridgeton, N. J.

The date of organization was March 1, 1894, with a voluntary secretary. Financial aid is secured by means of an annual membership fee of fifty cents from each member of the League, and a subscribed guaranty fund to be collected at such times and in such percentage amounts as the necessities of the treasury may require. The executive committee of twenty-five meets at the call of the chairman, to discuss the work of the League, subdivided into committees on:

1. Membership.
2. Finance.
3. Legislation.
4. Press.
5. Prosecution.
6. Audit.

There is no organ of the society. According to its constitution, "its purposes and objects shall be to encourage and assist the constituted authorities in maintaining law and order, and to promote the nomination and election to municipal offices of the men best qualified to serve the city, without regard to their party politics." The results already attained have been some twenty successful prosecutions tending to better respect for law. Women are not eligible to membership. The political action of the club is not restricted, as the League will undertake, in its organized capacity, to influence the nomination and election of candidates for municipal office whenever the executive committee shall determine by a vote of the majority of the whole committee that such action is advisable. In such a case it will act by indorsement or disapproval of candidates named by either party, either for the legislative or executive offices, or by offering its own candidates should such an extreme measure be necessary.

The movement began as a "law and order" society, following the declaration by the Supreme Court of New Jersey that the offensive excise legislation by the rum and race-track legislature of that State was unconstitutional. The League expected the licensed rum and saloon men to show fight, and so they did. They also undertook to carry on numberless "speak-easies," and it was against them that the work of prosecution was carried on, resulting in closing a great many of them in the city; but the League is greatly handicapped by the impossibility of getting away with the bottlers and distillers outside the city limits, who are not amenable to the city ordinance. Bridgeton is and has been for a good many years (except under the *régime* of the excise commissions) a no-license town.

When organizing the "law and order" society the question arose, "Why not enlarge the scope to the proportions of a Municipal League?" The constitution adopted looks to political action for the betterment of city government, but has never yet been put to the test of action. What the future of the organization may be, or if it is to have any, cannot now be said.

THE CITIZENS' PROTECTIVE ASSOCIATION

President,
GEORGE W. YOUNG.

Secretary,
A. L. REDDERS,
95 Nashville Avenue,
New Orleans, La.

The date of organization was May, 1894. The secretary's position is voluntary. Subscriptions support the Association, whose object, according to the constitution, is the protection of the citizens against any adverse legislation on the part of the City Council. An executive committee of seven holds weekly sessions and determines all measures brought before it. The Association has no organ of its own, but comes in touch with its workers by means of local boards in each of the seventeen wards. No member of the Association is permitted to be a candidate for any political office. Women are eligible to membership.

The actual results accomplished have been the indictment by the grand jury of ten councilmen and the beginning of impeachment proceedings against the mayor. One councilman was found guilty.

CITY CLUB OF HARTFORD

President,
   CHARLES E. GROSS.

Secretary,
   ARCHIBALD A. WELCH,
      Hartford, Conn.

The date of organization was 1894, under a voluntary secretary. According to the constitution, "its object shall be to stimulate and maintain an active interest among the citizens of Hartford in the government of their town and city in all their departments; to discuss methods and suggest and carry out plans for bringing about needed reforms in town and city governments; and to consider any other questions bearing on the welfare of the town and city of Hartford."

There is but one class of members. The dues are made $2 a year, in order that they may not form any excuse for not joining, and voluntary subscriptions, it is hoped, will make up the rest of the necessary expenses. The executive committee is composed of nine directors. These meet as often as once in two months, and frequently several times during a month, as necessity demands. There is but one standing committee—that on membership. There is no organ of the society, but the Club comes in contact with its members during the winter months by weekly meetings of the most informal kind, at which all members are welcome to come and express their views on any items of public interest. There are no minor organizations dependent upon the Club.

The constitution restricts the action of the Club to town and municipal government, and has nothing in it regarding the eligibility of women to membership. That question has not come before the Club as yet.

The Club was formed with the idea of keeping alive public interest in public affairs, and not with a view to overturning any ring in the city government. It seemed as if there were numerous reforms which were sadly needed, and which could only be brought about by a strong public opinion which could be expressed in some formal way. There has been awakened an interest in the affairs of the city which can be appreciated only by those who are citizens here, and at a recent meeting of the citizens the subject of asking the legislature to do away entirely with the county commissioners, who now have the granting of licenses among other duties, and who in the opinion of the citizens of this State have grossly misused this power, was referred to the Club, and the Club was instructed by the citizens of Hartford to take steps to secure the coöperation of other parts of the State, and to formulate a plan by which the powers of these commissioners could be distributed, and the office done away with.

CITY CLUB OF NEW BRUNSWICK

President,
DR. HENRY R. BALDWIN.

Secretary,
PROFESSOR L. BEVIER, JR.,
Rutgers College,
New Brunswick, N. J.

Date of organization, February 21, 1894. The position of the secretary is voluntary. Active members pay no dues, but sustaining members are assessed $10 each year. An executive committee is chosen by the Board of Managers from among their own number. This committee meets at least once a month. The following standing committees are appointed by the Board of Managers from among the members, and the chairman of each shall be a member of the Board of Managers:

    1. Membership.   3. Legislation.
    2. Audit.   4. Local Government.
                   5. Work.

The lowest unit of organization is the ward. The Club has no organ of its own. Women are not eligible to membership. Political action is not restricted, as members pledge themselves to nominate or indorse only such candidates as they believe to be honest and capable and in sympathy with the principle of absolute separation of local from State and national politics.

According to its constitution the objects of the Club are: "To eliminate all national and State politics from our local politics; to secure the nomination and election of candidates solely on account of their honesty and fitness for the office; to see that our local government be conducted upon non-partizan and strictly business principles; and to encourage every wise project for adding to the comfort and convenience of our citizens, and to the prosperity and development of our city."

In furtherance of those objects, at the spring election in 1894 it secured better nominations, hence better aldermen; and a spirit of greater independence in municipal elections was aroused.

THE CITY CLUB OF NEW YORK

President,
JAMES C. CARTER.

Secretary,
JAMES W. PRYOR,
27 Pine Street,
New York.

The organization of the Club was in 1892, and April 4th of the same year the society was incorporated. The secretary holds a salaried position. There are two classes of members, resident and non-resident. Annual dues of members and contributions to the "political fund" furnish financial support. The executive committee is composed of nine, and the officers of the Club *ex officio*, meeting once a week. The departments of work are:

1. Membership.
2. Audit.
3. House.
4. Library.
5. Legislative.
6. Municipal Government.
7. Coöperation and Affiliated Clubs.
8. Organization.
9. Publication and Records.

The Club has no organ of its own, but comes in touch with its members through its committees and the Good Government Clubs. The political action of the organization is restricted to municipal matters and non-partizan action. Women are ineligible to membership. According to its constitution the objects of the Club are: "To promote social intercourse among persons specially interested in promoting good government of the city of New York, in securing honesty and efficiency in the administration of city affairs, in severing municipal from national politics; and to take such action as may tend to the honest, efficient, and independent government of the city of New York."

The chief result has been the establishing of more than twenty Good Government Clubs, most of which are flourishing. In securing legislation and preparing important constitutional amendments the Club has taken an active part.

COMMITTEE OF PUBLIC SAFETY

President,
DAVID M. GREENE.

Secretary,
CHARLES I. BAKER,
Troy, N. Y.

Date of organization, March 8, 1894, with a voluntary secretary. The organization is supported by voluntary subscriptions, and has for its object "to investigate and endeavor to bring to the bar of justice all fraud in connection with the liberties of the people, especially crimes against the right of suffrage." An executive committee of fifteen meets when called by its chairman, and the following are the departments of work:

1. Attorneys.
2. Auditing.
3. Business.
4. Evidence.
5. Special Finance.
6. Grand Juries.
7. Legislation.
8. Public Sentiment.
9. Analysis of Vote.

The association is non-political, and women are not eligible to membership. The membership is limited to one hundred, and that number composed the Committee of Public Safety at its organization. The murder of Robert Ross while defending the purity of the ballot at an election in Troy, March 6, 1894, afforded the reason for the organization of the Committee. A good measure of success has rewarded its efforts, for it has secured good grand juries, better trial juries, conviction of election offenders, and awakened public conscience.

THE CITY GOVERNMENT CLUB

President,
H. O'SHEA.

Secretary,
D. P. DONOVAN,
1911 Pennsylvania Avenue,
Pittsburg, Pa.

This Club was organized May 1, 1893, with a voluntary secretary. According to the constitution, its object is to improve the city government and help obtain the best results for its citizens. An executive committee of nine meets each month. Women are eligible to membership, and the Club is not restricted in its political action. The secretary writes:

"We have accomplished a few good deeds so far, but they are hardly worth mentioning. One of them was the removal of a switch from the sidewalk in the Ninth Ward, and another the cleaning of a few of the streets and paving of the same in the Twelfth Ward."

CITY IMPROVEMENT SOCIETY

Secretary,
J. C. PUMPELLY,
12 East Twenty-third Street,
New York.

The date of the incorporation was June 14, 1892. An executive committee of six, known as a Managing Committee, meeting once a month, with a voluntary secretary, directs the work. There are two classes of members. Any person interested in the work of the Society may become a member. Active members subscribe $5 annually, and agree to watch the condition of the city and report matters deserving the attention of the Society. Associate members take no part in the work of the Society, but aid it by contributing toward its financial support in sums from $5 upward. The Society is not restricted in its political action, and women are eligible to membership.

A number of citizens interested in improving the condition of the city have organized this Society, and have given their time and labor to its service. It is strictly non-partizan in politics, and has met with the courteous and active coöperation of the heads of the different city departments. It has the active support and advice of physicians, civil and sanitary engineers, architects, and citizens of other professions; the daily papers have given their encouragement; and it endeavors to secure State and municipal legislation to effect needed improvements. It furnishes a medium never before existing, whereby a citizen having any complaint to make can be assured that his complaint will be presented to the proper authorities, in the proper manner, and will be looked after and pushed until it is attended to.

"Since the date of our last annual report [1894] the total number of complaints referred by us to the different city departments aggregate over forty-three hundred, embracing complaints of defective sidewalks, streets, sidewalk and roadway encumbrances, unclean streets, nuisances, etc. Of the total number of complaints forwarded to the departments up to March, 1894, about seventy-five per cent. have thus far been remedied, while, of course, of the additional number sent in 1894, with the exception of about three hundred relating to street and sidewalk encumbrances, nuisances, etc., a much smaller percentage have been attended to. These complaints relate to defective sidewalk and street pavements, which, as a rule, require from three to six months, or even longer, before any result can be obtained on which to base an estimate. Many of the objects, as outlined in our report, have already been accomplished, viz.: the placing of additional settees and the repairing and improvement of many of our parks; the more general training of the Japanese ivy; the repaving of many of the streets, and removal of permanent obstructions along same; the running of street-cars at regular intervals at night; the removal of news-stands and signs along the sidewalks of many of the principal avenues and thoroughfares; the securing of a new hack ordinance relating to the hanging of the rate-card, etc. The principal questions that at present engage our attention are: the cremation of the city's garbage; providing seats for female employees in stores; and a better tenement-house system. Our Society has also a membership in the State Municipal League and the Municipal Art Association. Our great success thus far has been due to the fact that we never antagonize any of the public officials or departments; we merely call their attention to the fact that the law bearing upon the question at issue is not enforced."

CITY REFORM CLUB

President,
W. HARRIS ROOME.

Secretary,
R. A. ZERGA,
New York.

This Club was organized about fifteen years ago, and had a membership of several hundred. All that is left of the original membership is an executive committee of fifteen. One very valuable contribution of this committee was the publication of the annual record of the New York Senators and Representatives in the legislature, under the title, "What Are You Going to Do about It?" It is a matter of sincere regret that this valuable contribution has been discontinued. From time to time this executive committee takes an active share in affairs needing the direction of public-spirited men. These men are all identified with the City Club and with the various Good Government Clubs.

THE CIVIC CLUB

President,
A. W. BURR.

Secretary,
E. S. GREENE,
Beloit, Wis.

The organization of the Club was effected February, 1893. December 28, 1892, some earnest men and women of Beloit met to discuss the plan of forming a Civic Club. The purposes of such a club were partially set forth in the call, as follows:

"OUR CIVIC WELFARE.

"The good people of Beloit have churches, have homes, have a business, but they also have a city. A good city binds every strand into a cable of power. A mean city untwists every good strand. To have a good city and keep it so earnest men and women must think over it, talk about it, and work toward it. .

"Through committees, reports, and discussions these five fingers of civic opportunity may be bound into one strong hand that shall be felt for good in all our loved Beloit, and in other cities also, we may hope. Every good man and woman living here is bound to be a good citizen of Beloit, an unselfish servant of the public weal."

After a general expression of opinion by those present, a committee of nine was appointed to formulate a plan of organization to be presented at a subsequent meeting. The plan of the committee was approved after some modifications, and the committee was instructed to call a larger meeting of those who might become charter members, and to nominate officers and committees for the Club. This meeting was held at Odd Fellows' Hall, February 22, 1893, when the organization of the Club was completed.

The Club is not incorporated, and the secretary holds a voluntary position. Financial support is obtained by an annual fee of $1. Seven members comprise the executive committee, who meet every two months to discuss the work of the Club, which falls under the following departments:

1. Civic Improvements and Civic Economy.
2. Education and Recreation.
3. Relief and Work.
4. Order and Law.
5. Civic Office and Civic Duty.

The Club has no organ of its own, but comes in touch with its members by means of its stated meetings and the press. There is no restriction on its political action, and women are eligible to membership. The object, as stated in the constitution, "shall be to promote the civic welfare of Beloit. Its work shall be to study and to better in every wise way the common conditions of the public weal.

"Its spirit shall be catholic, unpartizan, patriotic, and Christian. Its methods of work shall be through papers, reports, discussions, resolutions, public meetings, the press, committees, and the personal efforts of its members."

The largest result thus far accomplished is a more general awakening to the possibilities of civic life. Each committee has presented topics to the Club for thought and work. The results of the discussions have been printed in the press, whereby a widened circle of readers have been enabled to profit by the papers.

THE CIVIC FEDERATION OF CHICAGO.

President,
LYMAN J. GAGE.

Secretary,
RALPH M. EASLEY,
517 First National Bank Building,
Chicago, Ill.

The Federation was incorporated February 3, 1894. The secretary holds a salaried position. Financial aid is secured by subscriptions, as there are no membership fees. The executive committee consists of fifteen, meeting twice a month. According to the constitution, "the purposes of this Federation shall be:

"1. The formation of an influential, non-political, non-sectarian association, embracing all the forces that are now laboring to advance the municipal, philanthropic, industrial, and moral interests of Chicago, and to use and aid such forces in promoting the honesty, efficiency, and economy of its municipal government and the highest welfare of the citizens.

"2. To serve as a medium of acquaintance and sympathy between persons who reside in the different parts of the city, who pursue different vocations, who are by birth of different nationalities, who profess different creeds or no creed, who for any of these reasons are unknown to each other, but who, nevertheless, have similar interests in the well-being of Chicago, and who agree in the desire to promote every kind of municipal welfare.

"3. To increase the number and efficiency of agencies designed to discover and correct abuses in municipal affairs, and to increase the interest of the citizens in such affairs by securing the utmost practicable separation of municipal issues from State and national politics." .

The standing committees are:

1. Ways and Means.
2. Municipal.
3. Philanthropic.
4. Morals.
5. Educational.
6. Political.

Women are eligible to membership. There is a general council of one hundred men and women, plus the presidents of the ward councils. A council of fifty in each ward is known as the "ward council." Each precinct in the ward has a council, and the presidents of the precinct councils are also members of the ward council. Membership in the precinct council is unlimited. Any man or woman, of any race or religion, can become a member if the committee is satisfied that he or she is a good citizen and sincerely desires good government. Any member of any precinct or other council is eligible to the highest office in the gift of the Federation.

The work of the ward and precinct councils is the same as in the central council, and the same committees and subcommittees exist in these latter as in the central body. These subordinate councils are likewise composed of men and women of varying political beliefs. The Federation insists on all political parties being fully represented. It has happened that in a strongly Republican ward Republicans have been in a majority in the ward council, but it is equally true that in strongly Democratic wards the Democrats have had a majority in the council. As a rule, however, both parties are pretty evenly represented.

THE CIVIC FEDERATION OF DETROIT

Secretary,
REV. DONALD D. MACLAURIN.

At a meeting early in November, 1894, to consider the advisability of some kind of a reform organization, the above name was chosen and a temporary constitution adopted. According to it:

"The object of the Federation shall be to study the condition and needs of our city; to shape public opinion upon all questions relating to the municipal government; to organize the public conscience and bring it to bear upon existing evils; to separate municipal from State and national politics; to endeavor to secure the nomination and election of competent and trustworthy men for public office without respect to party lines; to this end to federate the moral forces of the city, and to promote in all ways the welfare, order, and prosperity of Detroit. The Federation seeks to accomplish these ends by the investigation of our municipal life; by agitation concerning existing evils; by the enforcement of present laws; by the securing of improved legislation; and by the massing of moral influence in behalf of municipal regeneration."

Branch Federations will be organized in any ward as soon as twenty-five members shall be secured, but the branch will only be recognized after the indorsement of the Central Committee.

The work of the Federation shall be divided into departments as follows:

1. Philanthropy.
2. Morals.
3. Education.
4. Temperance.
5. Social Evil.
6. Legislation.
7. Conferences.
8. Tenements.
9. Political.
10. Industrial.

These departments may be subdivided as the Central Committee may from time to time determine.

CIVIC FEDERATION OF GALESBURG

President,
W. E. TERRY.

Secretary,
GODFREY HASS,
Galesburg, Ill.

This Federation was organized October 1, 1894, under a voluntary secretary. The executive committee of eight meets once a month, and comes in touch with the workers by means of public meetings. The lowest municipal area which serves as the unit of organization is the election precinct. The Federation is not restricted in its political action, and women are eligible to membership. According to its constitution, the object of this organization "is to secure a thoroughly businesslike administration of the municipal affairs of our city, and the honest letting and fulfilling of contracts for public improvements; the enforcement of laws concerning gambling, prostitution, illegal selling of liquor, and Sunday observance. Matters concerning the public health and any destitution in our city shall also be objects to receive attention from this organization."

This Federation was organized for a definite purpose. Galesburg is a college city, with an abundance of schools, churches, and splendid homes. Gradually, yet surely, a vicious element was controlling the city. At the election in the spring of 1893, when the citizens' candidate was elected mayor by five votes, a change was made in one precinct and an apparent majority of seven was recorded for the liberal candidate. Thirteen votes were stolen somehow, and the will of the people defeated. In the summer of 1894 a race-track, with all the accompaniments of gambling and pool-selling, was opened, and an era of lawlessness began that appalled the people.

On Thursday of the race week, in pursuance of the demand of an outraged people, the county officials made a move that closed fourteen gambling-establishments. A call for all citizens who wished to band together and compel the mayor and officers to enforce the law brought together a number of solid citizens, and the Civic Federation was born. Fourteen indictments were brought against gaming-houses, and eleven convictions were secured. The organization numbers one hundred.

Among the results actually accomplished, the secretary states that gambling has been almost abolished, Sunday sale of liquor stopped, the removal of screens from saloons, and the awakening of the public sentiment.

COMMITTEE OF FIFTY

President,
GRANGE SOND.

Secretary,
JOHN W. McHONG,
446 Broadway,
Albany, N. Y.

At a mass-meeting held in the City Hall, November 13, 1893, the chairman was authorized to appoint a Committee of Fifty to consider what action should be taken to prevent the recurrence of fraudulent registration and voting at elections to be held hereafter in Albany, and to procure the passage of such legislation as will secure that result. The executive committee consists of five and the officers *ex officio*, who meet at the call of the chairman. The Committee is composed of twenty Democrats, twenty Republicans, three Independents, one Prohibitionist, and one Labor man. There are no standing committees, and the organization has no organ of its own. A voluntary secretary directs the work of the committee.

"Immediately following organization, November 15, 1893, an effort was made to punish the offenders at the past general election. Arrests were made of several police officials and of many minor political workers who had openly and flagrantly violated every law possible in connection with the election work; but witnesses and jurors were intimidated by the omnipresent authority of the ring, and not a single conviction was procured. This work filled the period up to the charter election in April, 1894. At that time a party organization was effected (Honest Elections party), embracing candidates both Democratic and Republican, and the Republican organization supported the same ticket.

"Earnest work was performed in purging the registry, and on election day at the polls, with the gratifying result of electing the entire city ticket and a controlling representation in the county and city boards. A healthy change in government is already evident both as to efficiency and economy. Obstacles have been put forward by both the ring Republicans and ring Democrats. Many arrests were made at the polls on election day, and a few strangers have been sent to prison for repeating and fraudulent voting, but we have yet been unable to convict a single important political worker. Our grand-jury system was very faulty; a new bill was passed by the last legislature, and the first grand jury under the new law will sit September 8, 1894. The district attorney has promised to make another effort to obtain indictments, but this official is still a relic of the Democratic ring, and at the coming fall election it is hoped that the work of reform will be extended to this office."

COMMITTEE OF PUBLIC SAFETY

President,
NATHAN COLE.

Secretary,
ISAAC LIMBERGER,
415 Locust Street,
St. Louis, Mo.

The Committee was organized November 16, 1894, after the election of that month, for the purpose of "a scathing investigation of frauds alleged to have been committed at the late city election." The secretary holds a voluntary position. The Committee will investigate alleged frauds practised by both party candidates; inquire into methods practised by recorder of voters, judges of election, and heelers; and suggest any needed reforms in election laws. The executive committee consists of four Republicans and four Democrats, and the president *ex officio*. The whole Committee consists of one hundred members, of both parties. Funds are solicited by the executive committee, and contributions made by members and others. A sufficient sum has already been raised to accomplish objects of association, and very satisfactory progress has been made. The Committee will be permanent and provide funds for prevention and punishment of frauds in future elections.

The executive committee meets at the call of the chairman, which has been about twice a week thus far. The Committee is unrestricted in its political action. Women are ineligible to membership. The animus of the organization is evident from this appeal:

"TO THE CITIZENS OF ST. LOUIS: From all quarters of the city, from members of all political parties, from the press, and from high officials, has come a demand for a searching, impartial, and non-partizan investigation of alleged fraudulent and criminal practices in the late election in this city. So specific have been these charges that the confidence of the community in the integrity as well as the adequacy of our election machinery has been impaired, and citizens and officials of all parties have united in demanding a broad, comprehensive, and non-partizan investigation. Realizing that this could not be secured, and the good name of the city vindicated, through unassisted individual contests, a number of citizens, representing all political views, have organized themselves as a Committee of Public Safety. The sole purpose of this organization is to meet this public demand for united and non-partizan action. The members have no private, personal, or partizan ends to serve. They realize that the safety of our institutions and all public and private right rests upon the integrity of the ballot-box in the expression of the popular will, and that the most dangerous of public enemies are those who violate its sanctity.

"This Committee has been organized by the election of Nathan Cole as president, Dr. William M. McPheeters and Daniel S. Holmes as vice-presidents, Isaac H. Limberger as secretary, and Cornelius Tompkins as treasurer.

"An executive committee has been provided, consisting of eight members, equally divided between the two leading political parties, to whom is delegated the carrying out of these purposes of their organization. It is the intention of this Committee to take every proper step which the means provided for their support will permit to secure a complete investigation of the late election of this city, and to this end, through counsel and other assistance, to take such part as may be proper in one or more election contests which may be instituted by candidates; not merely, so far as this Committee is concerned, that such assisted contestants may be successful, but that the evidence of frauds and crimes, if any such there be, wherever found, even if concealed in the ballot-boxes of any precinct of the city, may be brought to light—that the law may be vindicated; that the guilty, whoever they may be, may be punished to the full extent of the criminal law; and that the defects of the existing election methods may be disclosed, so that adequate means may be provided by legislation for the ascertainment of the popular will.

"The extent and completeness of this work is dependent upon the means placed at our disposal. The Committee believes that all that is needed in this behalf in this emergency is an appeal to the citizens of St. Louis, so that the necessary steps can be immediately taken and vigorously prosecuted. A large sum of money will be required, for which a strict account will be rendered. Contributions may be sent to Cornelius Tompkins, treasurer, at the office of the Union Trust Company. The Committee believes that the citizens of St. Louis will not permit the public trust which has been put upon them to fail for lack of the necessary support. The urgency of the situation demands promptness.

"NATHAN COLE, *President*,   I. W. MORTON,
GEORGE A. MADILL,   FREDERICK N. JUDSON,
GEORGE E. LEIGHTON,   BRECKINRIDGE JONES,
JACOB FURTH,   GAIUS PADDOCK,
STEPHEN A. BEMIS."

COMMITTEE OF SEVENTY

Chairman,
JOSEPH LAROCQUE.

Secretary,
JOHN P. FAURE,
238 West Eleventh Street,
New York.

This Committee was organized in September, 1894, as a culmination of the reform sentiment that concerted and definite action was necessary to secure good government. September 6th about seven hundred citizens assembled in the Madison Square Garden Concert-hall, in response to a circular of invitation signed by William E. Dodge, Gustav H. Schwab, and Hugh N. Camp. The meeting was organized under the temporary chairmanship of Joseph Larocque, with John P. Faure as secretary. According to a resolution then passed, this circular letter was issued:

"NEW YORK, September 8, 1894.

"DEAR SIR: At the conference of citizens held at the Madison Square Garden Concert-hall on Thursday, 6th instant, for the purpose of consulting as to the wisdom of organizing a citizens' movement for the government of the city of New York, entirely outside of party politics, and solely in the best interests of efficiency, economy, and the public health, comfort, and safety, it was unanimously decided to take such action, and a resolution was adopted instructing the chairman of the conference to appoint a Committee of Seventy for the purpose of conferring with other anti-Tammany organizations, and of carrying out the objects of the meeting.

"Subject to your approval, your name has been selected as one of the members of that Committee, and I am instructed by the chair to inquire whether you would be willing to accept that position, and to express the hope that you will not withhold your assistance in the present emergency that imperatively calls for action on the part of the citizens of this metropolis."

The executive committee was thirty-one in number, meeting at the call of the chairman. Standing committees were appointed on:

1. Finance.
2. Executive.
3. Meetings.
4. Platform.
5. Speakers.
6. Press.
7. Legislation.
8. Practical Reform.

Women were ineligible to membership. In the manifesto sent out by the Platform Committee the issues were clearly stated:

"We reiterate the following principles, contained in the Address to the People of the City of New York, heretofore issued:

"Municipal government should be entirely divorced from party politics and from selfish personal ambition or gain.

"The economical, honest, and businesslike management of municipal affairs has nothing to do with questions of national or State politics.

"We do not ask any citizen to give up his party on national

or State issues, but to rise above partizanship to the broad plane of citizenship, and to unite in an earnest demand for the nomination and election of fitting candidates, whatever their national party affiliations.

"The government of the city of New York, in the hands of its present administrators, is marked by corruption, inefficiency, and extravagance; its municipal departments are not conducted in the interests of the city at large, but for private gain and partizan advantage.

"All classes of citizens, rich and poor alike, suffer under these conditions. This misgovernment endangers the health and morality of the community, and deprives its citizens of the protection of life and property to which they are entitled.

"The call goes to the citizens of New York to face the dangers that confront them, and resolutely to determine that these conditions shall cease and that the affairs of the city shall henceforth be conducted as a well-ordered, efficient, and economical household, in the interests of the health, comfort, and safety of the people.

"We denounce as repugnant to the spirit and letter of our institutions any discriminations among citizens because of race or religious belief.

"We demand that the public service of this city be conducted upon a strictly non-partizan basis; that all subordinate appointments and promotions be based on civil-service examinations, and that all examinations, mental and physical, be placed under the control of the Civil-service Commission.

"We demand that the quality of the public schools be improved, their capacity enlarged, and proper playgrounds provided, so that every child within the ages required by law shall have admission to the schools, the health of the children be protected, and that all such modern improvements be introduced as will make our public schools the equal of those in any other city in the world.

"We insist that the property already acquired by the city under the Small Parks Act shall be promptly devoted to the purposes of this acquisition, so that our people in the densely populated parts of our city shall fully enjoy the benefits of such expenditures.

"We urge greater care and thoroughness in the enforcement of the health laws, and demand the establishment of more efficient safeguards against disease.

"We favor the establishment of adequate public baths and lavatories for the promotion of cleanliness and increased public comfort, at appropriate places throughout the city.

"We demand the adoption of a thorough system of street-cleaning, which shall also include a proper disposition of the refuse and garbage, so that our harbor may be kept free from obstruction and defilement, and the neighboring shores clear of offal, thus conforming to the methods in other great cities.

"We call for increased rapid-transit facilities in this city.

"We call for the improvement of the docks and water-fronts of our great maritime city, so that it shall enjoy the advantages to which it is entitled by its unique position with its unrivaled harbor.

"We heartily favor the separation of municipal from State and national elections, and a larger measure of home rule for cities.

"We appeal to the people of this city to cast aside party prejudice and to combine with us in a determined effort to elect candidates chosen solely with reference to their ability and integrity, and pledged to conduct the affairs of this city on a strictly non-partizan basis, and who will, as far as may be in their power, insure good government to the city of New York."

The Committee of Seventy was selected so as to secure the most representative men in the community. Lists were prepared of the leading merchants, bankers, lawyers, business men, and associations of organized labor. From these lists the seventy were chosen. The whole history of the Committee thus far has confirmed the wisdom of the selection, for the men have worked harmoniously and with a singleness of purpose. The Committee was called together in the latter part of September to effect a permanent organization, when the officers, as named above, were chosen.

The Committee had shown what it could do in uniting the friends of good government by the splendid victory of November 6th, but it very well knew that this triumph was only a beginning, and that the enemy was rallying his forces on the day after the election. The Committee realized that its work must be continued, and that it owed it to the community to fulfil its ante-election demands, because previous to the election it had insisted that certain abuses must be reformed, and that other definite lines of work must be undertaken. In the pursuance of this purpose a committee of five was selected from the executive committee, under the chairmanship of Mr. A. C. Bernheim, and power given it to organize sub-committees to take under advisement the subjects of Street-cleaning, Garbage Disposal, Improvement of the Water-front, Civil Service, Public Baths and Lavatories, Small Parks, Tenement-house Reform, and Investigation of the Pay-rolls. The following was the resolution sanctioning the appointment of the above committees:

"WHEREAS, The platform of the Committee of Seventy demands the introduction of public improvements, such as small parks, baths, and lavatories; and

"WHEREAS, That platform condemned the administration of Tammany officials, because they failed to undertake such improvements, and at the same time wasted the public moneys through corrupt expenditures and supplies and salaries; and

"WHEREAS, This Committee believes that this waste will be found sufficient to, in large measure, defray the expense of these public improvements without much addition to the city tax-levy; therefore be it

"*Resolved*, That a committee of five be appointed by the chair to prepare a plan in detail of such improvements, and to investigate the expenditure of public moneys for supplies and salaries; . . . to report its conclusion to this executive committee, and to have power to associate with itself others, in an advisory capacity, and to fill vacancies."

It was the plan that each of these sub-committees should be composed of experts who were perfectly familiar with the subject under discussion, and should prepare a report to contain their recommendations, which will be finally submitted to the mayor for such action as he may see fit. To illustrate the formation of these committees: Mr. John P. Faure, from his experience of twenty years in connection with the Floating Hospital of the St. John's Guild, and from his practical knowledge of the needs of the people, was charged with the formation of the group to discuss the subject of Baths and Lavatories. His selection for chairman was eminently fitting, in the appointment of William Gaston Hamilton, who has made such a splendid success of the People's Baths at Center Market, in connection with the Association for Improving the Condition of the Poor. The work of this committee will require a very much longer space of time because the subjects have received but the merest consideration in this country, and, for that matter, the ample provisions that are being made for them in Continental cities are of very recent date. It is the aim of this committee to embody in its report a comparative study of the existing provisions in American municipalities and those of the English cities; it will show what the city of New York is doing to meet these requirements; and it will conclude by making certain concrete definite recommendations. There is no reason why this and the other reports should not be models and summaries of the very latest information concerning these important phases of the civic welfare of a nineteenth century municipality.

COUNCIL OF CONFEDERATED GOOD GOVERNMENT CLUBS.

President,
J. AUGUSTUS JOHNSON.

Secretary,
PREBLE TUCKER,
110 Trinity Building,
111 Broadway,
New York.

"We, the Good Government Clubs of the city of New York, desiring to promote more effectively our common interests in good city government, do hereby agree with one another to take united action in all matters affecting our common interests, and for that purpose do by these presents establish this constitution for the Confederated Good Government Clubs."

The Council is composed of representatives of the various Good Government Clubs in the city of New York. This Council was organized in March, 1894, under a constitution which had previously been ratified by the Good Government Clubs then in the Confederation. The Council is not incorporated, although the Clubs composing the Confederation and sending representatives to the Council are incorporated. There were originally four Clubs in the Confederation; there are now seventeen, with four more Clubs organized but not yet admitted to the Confederation. The secretary does not hold a salaried position.

Each Club admitted to the Confederation pays annual dues at the rate of $15 for each representative it sends to the Council. The Clubs are entitled to send representatives as follows: each Club of fifty electors shall be entitled to one representative; each Club of one hundred electors shall be entitled to two representatives, and to one additional representative for each additional one hundred and fifty electors. No Club is entitled to more than six representatives.

The Council has regular meetings once a month, and is divided into standing committees as follows:

    1. Rules.
    2. Ways and Means.
    3. Organization and Conference.
    4. Formation and Admission of Good Government Clubs.
    5. Literature and the Press.
    6. Legislation.

In addition to this there are special committees appointed from time to time for special purposes.

The Confederation at present has no organ, although it publishes from time to time pamphlets upon different subjects connected with municipal reform.

The Council comes in touch with the workers through its Committee on Organization and Conference. This committee meets the chairmen of the various campaign committees of the Clubs. Each Club has a Campaign Committee, which looks after the workers in its district and appoints the captains of the various election districts. The lowest unit of organization is the Assembly district, although each Club appoints one or more workers in each election district in its Assembly district.

The Good Government Clubs are not restricted in their political action, except in so far that they confine themselves to municipal matters. The work of each Club is semi-educational and semi-political. The educational work is carried on by each Club, according to its facilities, through local committees. Its political work is carried on through a convention elected as provided in the constitution of the Confederation.

Several of the Clubs have also either nominated or indorsed

candidates for the Assembly in their respective districts, and propose to do so again. In several cases they also expect to nominate aldermen.

Women are not eligible to membership, although several of the Clubs have the active coöperation of women, who aid their committees in special work where their assistance is of value.

The work of the Council up to this time has been mainly in enlarging the number of Clubs and preparing the public mind to support a non-partizan municipal ticket. During the last election the Council was not in existence, but several of the Clubs nominated candidates for Assembly, and in two instances, with the aid of the Republican organization, elected them.

The origin of the Good Government Club movement belongs primarily to the work of the special committee of the City Club known as the Committee on Affiliated Clubs. The object of the Clubs is to obtain better municipal government. The first Club formed was in March, 1893. Since that time the Clubs have been growing in number and increasing in membership, until at the present time there are about six thousand duly elected members, who pay dues ranging from twenty-five to fifty cents a month.

GOOD GOVERNMENT CLUB A.*

President,
W. HARRIS ROOME.

Secretary,
A. H. GUTMAN,
15 Wall Street,
New York.

February, 1893, was the date of organization, and March 2, 1893, that of incorporation. A voluntary secretary directs the work. The membership dues are $6 a year. According

---

* This Club has been selected as typical of the rest, because it is the oldest and one of the most active.

to the articles of incorporation, "the particular business or object of such society or club shall be to promote social intercourse among persons specially interested in the good government of the city of New York, in securing honesty and efficiency in the administration of city affairs, in severing municipal from national politics, and in procuring the nomination and election of fit persons to city offices; and to take such action as may tend to the honest, efficient, and independent government of the city of New York; and for these purposes to establish and maintain in the city and county of New York, for the use of ourselves and such others above mentioned, suitable club accommodations."

The board of trustees, twenty in number, are an executive committee, who meet once a month. There are standing committees on:

1. Membership.
2. House.
3. Audit.
4. Library.
5. Entertainment.
6. District Improvement.
7. Legislation.
8. Campaign.
9. Press and Literature.
10. Study and Investigation of Street-cleaning.

Good Government Club A moved into its club-house in May, 1893. It is a social club of men who wish to be freed from packed and dishonest primaries at home and constant interference in city affairs by the legislature at Albany; they desire separate municipal elections, a blanket ballot without the blanket paster, and home rule, to the end that they may obtain the best possible municipal government, irrespective of party, at a fair cost.

The club-house is situated on the northwest corner of Lexington Avenue and Fifty-eighth Street. There is a well-equipped billiard-room in the basement. The parlor floor is neatly and comfortably furnished, and affords a convenient and attractive place of meeting for the members. Every two weeks meetings are held here, at some of which addresses are made by men familiar with city affairs and needs, followed by general discussion among the members. At other meetings entertainments of some kind, as music, recitations, "smokers," are given. The rooms on the second floor are fitted up as smoking and reading rooms, and have a supply of daily morning and evening papers, and magazines. Vienna Hall, holding six hundred persons, adjacent to the club-house and accessible through it, is at the service of the Club, at a nominal price, for large meetings for social or political purposes.

As a club, Club A is not intended to be anti-Democratic or anti-Republican, but to be persistently, consistently, and impartially anti-bad-city-government, and nothing else.

It has nothing to do with Tammany as such, nor with the Republican machine as such; but it has to do with the administrators of our city government as such, whoever they may be, and with the law, system, and methods under and in accordance with which or in violation of which that government is administered.

Among the results actually accomplished by the Club, the secretary mentions the prevention to a large extent of corruption at the polls, by means of a corps of watchers; the awakening of the public sentiment to the needs of city government; and the nomination of better men to public office.

GOOD GOVERNMENT CLUBS.

CLUB A, A. L. Gutman, Secretary, 15 Wall Street.
CLUB B, T. A. Fulton, Secretary, 70 West 104th Street.
CLUB C, Lewis C. King, Secretary, 253 West 88th Street.
CLUB D, Charles Taber, Secretary, 26 Exchange Place.
CLUB E, Edwin Emerson, Assistant Secretary, 338 East 23d Street.

CLUB F, John P. Faure, Secretary, 238 West 11th Street.
CLUB G, G. F. S. Allen, Secretary, 220 West 43d Street.
CLUB H, J. T. Morris, Secretary, 263 West 34th Street.
CLUB K, Max Cohn, Secretary.
CLUB L, Paul Kistel, Secretary, 350 East 85th Street.
CLUB M, Julius Steinberger, Secretary, 311 East 72d Street.
CLUB N, Louis Lichter, Secretary, 336 East 90th Street.
CLUB O, William W. Locke, Secretary, 126 East 28th Street.
CLUB P, F. C. Leubuscher, Secretary, 280 Broadway.
CLUB Q, Carl Pfeiffer, Secretary, 498 West 153d Street.
CLUB R, Albert L. Willis, Secretary, 8 Hampden Street.
CLUB S, Organizing.
CLUB T, Organizing. Gregory Weinstein, Secretary care of Club A.
CLUB U, James P. Heath, Secretary, 317 East 68th Street.
CLUB V, Louis Inman, Secretary, 136 Liberty Street.
CLUB W, Thomas H. Friend, Secretary, 32 Nassau Street.
CLUB X, M. J. Katz, Secretary, 201 Henry Street.
CLUB TENTH ASSEMBLY DISTRICT, Charles H. Kelvy, Secretary, 120 Broadway.

THE GOOD CITIZENSHIP EDUCATIONAL LEAGUE OF OMAHA.

President,
JAY BURNS.

Secretary,
J. O. DETWEILER,
508 Paxton Block,
Omaha, Neb.

Organized in August, 1894, this League has for its object, according to its constitution, "the education of the Christian people of Omaha in the conditions and needs of our city, and their duties as citizens to its municipal government." In order to educate the public conscience, and to secure a more generous support for all municipal movements which make for the public welfare, the League plans the study of the problems of municipal government (1) by classes and lectures for members; (2) by mass-meetings for the public; (3) by the study and circulation of literature bearing on the subject. An executive committee of seven meets regularly once a month. Women are eligible to membership.

The League is restricted in political action as it is organized at present; while it will do all in its power to awaken and stimulate the public conscience, it will leave political action to the organizations already in the field and outside of the church. The League's motto might be phrased, *Educate, agitate, coöperate.*

GOOD GOVERNMENT CLUB OF BERKELEY.

President,
THOMAS ADDISON.

Secretary,
ANSON S. BLAKE,
2222 Durant Avenue,
Berkeley, Cal.

April 7, 1894, this Club was organized, under a voluntary secretary. According to its constitution, "the objects of this Club shall be to keep before our citizens the necessity of their interest in public affairs; to discuss and shape public opinion upon all questions which relate to the proper government of Berkeley; to separate municipal from State and national politics; to secure the nomination and election of municipal officers solely on account of their fitness for the office; to federate for these purposes the various moral forces of the town; and to encourage every wise project for the promotion of the good order, prosperity, and honor of Berkeley."

The dues are $2 a year, and in addition voluntary subscriptions. An executive committee of five meets monthly. The departments of work are:

1. Grievance.   3. Town Officials.
2. Light and Water.   4. Streets.
      5. Mill Liquor Law.

The Club has no organ of its own, but issues occasional publications. The secretary writes:

"The town of Berkeley is composed of two very distinct portions: the West End, inhabited by loafers and a poor and rather vicious class of laborers, who are in Berkeley most of the time; and the East End, inhabited by a cultivated and intelligent class of people, whose business is for the most part in San Francisco and Oakland, the exceptions to the above rule being the professors (about one hundred and twenty-five) and students (about thirteen hundred) of the University of California, which is situated in the East End. Although the voting population of the East End is about two to one to that of the West End, that end of town has always dominated the other in things political, and Berkeley has had a remarkably poor government for a town whose population has such a large proportion of citizens of high moral standards. This state of affairs has always been deplored, but regarded as hopeless; but this spring several of the older inhabitants, and two or three recent comers from the Eastern States who were in touch with the movements for municipal reform there, met and decided to attempt an organization. We wrote to various organizations for suggestions, and called a meeting of forty citizens of Berkeley, who subsequently organized. Our membership list has been increased to ninety-five, and is limited to one hundred and fifty. Our object is to attain good municipal government for Berkeley by all means in our power—by educating first ourselves and then the public in matters of public welfare and government, so that the taste of the community will be for that sort of thing, and they will demand it; and in the meantime we shall endeavor to force the position of any who attempt anything contrary to the public good, and use our influence to bring the better portion of the community into active participation in matters of municipal politics. These are a few of our many ways proposed and in use to attain our one object, which is expressed in the name of the Club."

Among the results actually accomplished are: the successful blocking of several measures that were brought before the town trustees by the saloon-keepers; the appointment of a good board of trustees to frame a better charter; and an increase of about fifteen per cent. of the voters at the last election.

GOOD GOVERNMENT CLUB OF YONKERS

President,
HON. NORTON P. OTIS.

Secretary,
RALPH EARLE PRIME, JR.,
25 Warburton Avenue,
Yonkers, N. Y.

This Club was organized in 1894, with a voluntary secretary. As stated in its constitution, "the Good Government Club of Yonkers is organized to promote honest, efficient, and economical government in the city of Yonkers, and will welcome to its membership all citizens, without distinction of party, who are in sympathy with its purposes." Financial support is derived from the annual dues of members, $5. The management and control of the Club is vested in a board of fifteen trustees. Their regular meetings are held once each month, but special meetings may be held subject to the call of the president. There are three standing committees:

1. Membership. 2. Municipal Government. 3. Legislation.

There is no official organ of the Club; a ward committee consults for the interests of the Club in the five wards of the city. As to the part to be taken in political action by the Club this statement is made: "It is not the business, nor is it the desire, of this Club to weaken any man's allegiance to his State and national party, but it is one of the chief aims of the Club to weaken the influence of partizan politics in the government of the city of Yonkers." Women are not eligible to membership. Among the results actually accomplished by the Club are: a circular of definite and detailed information concerning the financial condition of the town; limitation of the contingent fund to $100,000; reconstruction of the Board of Health, making the health-officer the executive officer of the board, appointed by the board, and amenable to it, instead of being president, as at present; insertion of the word "wilfully" in the provision of the charter relating to obstruction of sidewalks, restricting the amount of bonds the Commissioner of Public Works may ask of the Common Council, without act of the legislature, to $10,000 in any one year; providing that no city official shall hold two offices; the desired change in the method of opening streets.

THE INTERNATIONAL LAW AND ORDER LEAGUE

President,
HON. CHARLES C. BONNEY.

Secretary,
PROFESSOR CLARENCE GREELEY,
Berkeley Temple,
Boston, Mass.

December 22, 1883, the League was organized, and its work is under the direction of a voluntary secretary. Its object is "to promote the enforcement of law through existing machinery, and to reform the laws when necessary." Voluntary subscriptions support the work. An executive committee of twelve meets once each month. The organ of the League is the *City Vigilant* and *Lend a Hand.* The organization is non-partizan, and women are ineligible to membership. The organization was effected in Tremont Temple, when delegates from the Law and Order Leagues in eight States met in conference. The name International was adopted at a subsequent meeting in Toronto. Its work is mainly educational, and consists in holding public meetings and in giving wide currency to the addresses.

CITIZENS' LAW AND ORDER LEAGUE

President,
HON. JOSEPH R. HAWLEY.

Secretary,
SAMUEL P. THRASHER,
102 Orange Street,
New Haven, Conn.

The date of organization was September 28, 1892, with a salaried secretary. "The object of this League shall be to secure, by all proper means, the enforcement of existing laws." Voluntary subscriptions supply the financial aid. The executive committee of nine meets at the call of the secretary. The *Connecticut Citizen* is the organ of the League. The society is not restricted in its political action. Women are eligible to membership. Among the results actually accomplished has been the conviction of nearly three hundred lawbreakers.

THE LIBRARY HALL ASSOCIATION OF CAMBRIDGE

President,
RICHARD H. DANA.

Secretary,
GEORGE G. WRIGHT,
86 Mt. Auburn Street,
Cambridge, Mass.

Organization was effected December 18, 1889, but as yet no incorporation. No compensation is paid to any of the officials. An annual fee of $1, and voluntary contributions from those who are interested in its work, furnish the financial support. The executive committee consists of twenty-eight, meeting as often as the exigencies of the society demand. There are no standing, but special committees. At election time a campaign paper is mailed to each voter. This contains a brief sketch of all the candidates, with any other matter which the committee may issue. It is sent to every voter on the revised lists. "Any citizen of Cambridge shall be eligible to membership without regard to his political preferences. Proposals for membership shall be made in writing to the executive committee in such form as they may provide, and if approved by three fourths of that committee the applicant shall become a member upon signing these by-laws and payment of the admission fee. Proposals not approved by the executive committee may be referred by any member to the Association, which may, by a three-fourths vote of all present at any meeting, elect said applicant."

The Association has accomplished the election of good men by means of previous indorsement after a careful study of their records. Thus, in 1893, the Association indorsed eleven aldermen and nine of them were elected; twenty members of the Common Council were indorsed and eighteen elected; while five school-committee men were indorsed and all were elected. Many citizens have come to look to the Association for guidance, because it has won their confidence through previous wisdom and fairness. According to its constitution, "the purposes of the Association shall be to secure the nomination and election of proper candidates for municipal offices; to procure the punishment of all persons who may be guilty of election frauds, maladministration of office, or misappropriation of public funds; to advocate and promote a public service based upon character and capability only; and to promote intelligent discussion of municipal affairs by the publication and distribution of reliable information in relation thereto."

MASSACHUSETTS SOCIETY FOR PROMOTING GOOD CITIZENSHIP

Honorary President,
    EDWARD EVERETT HALE.

Secretary,
    RAY GREENE HARDING,
        Boston, Mass.

In December, 1887, a circular letter signed by a dozen Boston gentlemen was distributed to those who presumably might be interested in its subject. It began as follows: "Three existing conditions threaten the stability of our republican institutions. The first of these is the prevalent indifference among instructed American citizens to the observance of their duties as such, and their apparent forgetfulness of the principles upon which those duties are based. The second is the greater or less ignorance of those principles and duties which prevails among a very large class of citizens, especially those of foreign birth. The third is the avowed, deliberate purpose of a large number of citizens, and of residents who are not citizens, to change our present time-honored form of citizenship for other and experimental forms. . . . All who desire the perpetuity of our institutions must admit that it is necessary to arouse the first-named from their indifference, to instruct the second, and to combat the intentions of the third."

The circular proposed the formation of a society to carry out these purposes; and in response to its suggestions the Massachusetts Society for Promoting Good Citizenship was organized, December 20, 1887. The services of the secretary are voluntary. According to its constitution, "the object of this Society shall be to disseminate a knowledge of the principles of good citizenship, and to promote the observance of the duties imposed thereby." There is an annual membership fee of $1.

An executive committee consists of seven, while there are the following standing committees:

1. Membership.
2. Courses of Study.
3. Publications and Lectures.
4. Finance.

The work actually accomplished has been the courses of lectures by the Society, delivered upon municipal topics by those who were most fitted to speak on these topics.

THE MEN'S PATRIOTIC GUILD

President,
J. F. HENRICI.

Secretary,
WILLIAM P. FLINT,
3301 Fifth Avenue,
Pittsburg, Pa.

The date of organization was November 26, 1893. There are no paid officers. According to its constitution:

"The objects of this society shall be:

"1. To promote the knowledge of its members in all matters pertaining to the history, laws, and politics of our nation, State, and city, and to encourage the application of ethical principles to political practice in all branches of our government.

"2. To coöperate with the First Unitarian Church of Pittsburg in carrying out all its social and charitable activities."

The Guild endeavors to obtain active members from among people who are in no way interested in the church, and, in fact, has some such members at present. In their case the first object of the society is the only one to which they are considered subscribers. This object is the dominant one, and questions coming under the head of the second object rarely take up more than ten minutes of the Guild's time at any meeting.

The funds for current expenses are raised by assessments, and extraordinary expenses are defrayed by voluntary contributions. A managing committee of three directs the affairs of the organization. Political action is unrestricted. Women are ineligible to membership. Among the results actually accomplished, the Guild aided Kingsley House by furnishing workers to take hold of the work of that college settlement under the direction of its residents. Kingsley House is located in the mill district of Pittsburg, and is managed by a board of directors representing many different Christian denominations. In conjunction with Kingsley House the Guild arranged a free lecture by Herbert Welsh on "Good City Government," and one by Clinton Rogers Woodruff on "Obstacles to Good Government."

MUNICIPAL ASSOCIATION

President,
J. W. DAVIDSON.

Secretary,
DANIEL KILHAM DODGE,
University of Illinois,
Champaign, Ill.

This Association was organized in 1893, for the "promotion of municipal affairs," and is not incorporated. The position of the secretary is voluntary. An executive committee of four, with no stated times for meeting, directs the work, divided into five departments:

1. General.
2. Hygiene.
3. Police.
4. Fire and Lighting.
5. Laws.

There is no organ of the society, but public meetings enable the Association to come in touch with those who are interested. The membership fee is $1 a year. There is no part taken by the Association in the nomination or election of officials. Women are ineligible to membership. The secretary states that among the results already accomplished is an aroused interest in sewerage and public-school sanitation.

The Association originated in the meetings of the local Ministers' Association, composed of the ministers of all the churches, with the exception of the Roman Catholic and the

Episcopalian. Certain laymen were invited to coöperate with them in their endeavor. At a meeting of about a dozen persons, held in November, 1892, a preliminary organization was formed, which developed into the present Association. The membership consists of the ministers of the eight Protestant churches and four members from each of these churches, selected by the ministers. To these were added ten members at large.

MUNICIPAL CLUB OF DECATUR

President,
    WILLIAM H. STARR.

Secretary,
    H. P. PAGE,
    Decatur, Ill.

The date of organization was October 9, 1894. The services of the secretary are voluntary. The executive committee of sixteen meets twice a month. As the organization is so recent the departments of work have not yet been determined. There is no restriction on the political action of the Club. According to its constitution:

"We, the members of the Municipal Club of Decatur, inviting the coöperation of all our fellow-citizens, hereby declare and pledge ourselves to the enforcement of the following principles:

"1. We, as citizens of Decatur, believe that our highest interests will be materially promoted by the absolute separation of municipal government from national and State politics.

"2. Realizing that respect for law is the bulwark of liberty, we demand a vigorous observance and enforcement of all our laws, and we pledge ourselves to nominate or indorse only such candidates as we believe to be in favor of such enforcement, honest, and capable of properly administering the affairs of our municipal government.

"3. We advocate practical extension of the highest principles of civil-service reform to our municipal departments.

"4. It will be the special object of the Municipal Club of Decatur to make a thorough and scientific investigation of the correct principles of local self-government, especially as adapted to this municipality, and to collect and publish all appropriate information on the defects and needs of the city government. While the members of this Club may be members of widely different national and State organizations, all will be united in the common purpose of obtaining the best city government and the wisest expenditure of money, of advancing the material growth of this municipality, and of stimulating that spirit of progress in her citizens which will secure for them and their descendants the largest measure of domestic comfort and commercial prosperity."

Results actually accomplished are precluded by the extreme youth of the Club, but there is a membership of about six hundred, and the intention of the Club is to place a non-partizan ticket in the field at the spring election of city officers. The action of the Club has already disturbed the old-line politicians, and the subject of "city government is business—not politics" will be given an airing.

MUNICIPAL CLUB OF ROCHESTER

Secretary,
ISAAC ADLER,
811 Wilder Building,
Rochester, N. Y.

The constitution was adopted in June, 1894, when a few gentlemen interested in good government met to discuss the formation of a Good Government Club. A meeting was held June 29, 1894, at which a dozen or fifteen gentlemen were present. A constitution which follows substantially that of the Good Government Clubs of New York was adopted. October 16th a second meeting was held, at which some thirty or forty were present. Most of those present became members of the Club. A board of trustees was elected at this meeting, and addresses were listened to from Mr. Nathaniel Bacon, of the Syracuse Good Government Club, and others. The organization will be perfected as soon as possible, and the work of the Club begun. The annual dues are $1. The executive committee cannot be less than five in number, and three of the five must be trustees. It meets at the call of the chairman.

The objects of the society, as stated in its constitution, are: (1) to secure the nomination and election of proper candidates for municipal offices, and the selection of fit persons for positions filled by appointment; (2) to procure the punishment of any persons who may attempt frauds affecting elections, or who may be guilty of maladministration of office or misappropriation of public funds; (3) to advocate and promote a public service based upon character and capacity only; and (4) to promote intelligent discussion of municipal affairs by the collection, publication, and distribution of reliable information in relation thereto.

The Club has no organ of its own, and is not restricted in its political action. As its formation is so recent no definite results can be yet reported, but the educational features of the organization will be sure to secure a higher municipal tone.

MUNICIPAL IMPROVEMENT ASSOCIATION OF KANSAS CITY

President,
   AUGUST R. MYER.

Secretary,
   W. B. RICHARDS,
      Fifth and Wyandotte Streets,
         Kansas City, Mo.

The date of organization was January 2, 1892, and of incorporation, January 28, 1892. The secretary holds a voluntary position. According to the constitution, the Association is organized (1) for the accumulation and study of all such information and statistics from the experience of other cities as may have a bearing upon methods of levying public taxes, upon the expenditure of public moneys, upon the establishment and maintenance of public parks and boulevards, upon paving sidewalks and street-cleaning, upon water and gas service, upon sewerage and sanitation, upon the laying out of additions, upon all forms of intramural transportation, and upon every department of municipal government and usage; (2) to take such vigorous and effective measures, by the use of the information so obtained, to secure the coöperation of all good citizens in publishing and promoting every measure of improvement and reform which may benefit Kansas City, and to secure for its inhabitants all the advantages to be obtained in the wise and economical administration of its affairs; (3) to secure the passage of such ordinances as will promote the health, comfort, and safety of the community, and to this end to secure the enforcement, modification, or repeal, as the case may require, of city ordinances and State laws relating to municipalities.

Regular meetings of the executive committee of ten are held twice each month. There are standing committees on:

1. Methods of Levying Public Taxes.
2. Expenditure of Public Money.
3. Establishing and Maintaining Public Parks and Boulevards.
4. Paving Sidewalks and Street-cleaning.
5. Water and Gas Service.
6. Sewerage and Sanitation.
7. Laying Out of Additions.
8. All Forms of Intramural Transportation.
9. Every Department of Municipal Government and Usage.

The Association is not restricted in its political action, and women are ineligible to membership. The Association places its investigations and discussions at the disposal of the public and the officials through the press, and urges the enforcement of such laws as are neglected by the municipal government, particularly in the health and street departments.

Among the results already accomplished the secretary mentions the passage of a good park and boulevard law, investigation and betterment of conditions at city hospital, wakening sentiment in favor of the parks and boulevards and of the separation of the city from the county government.

THE MUNICIPAL LEAGUE OF GRAND RAPIDS

President,
   CHARLES R. SLIGH.

Secretary,
   WILLIAM H. KINSEY,
      Grand Rapids, Mich.

May 15, 1894, the League was organized, with a voluntary secretary. Voluntary contributions support the League, which has this purpose:

"The objects of the League shall be to awaken and enlist the sympathy and active interest of all good citizens in the municipal affairs of Grand Rapids, hoping thereby that none but honest and competent persons will be elected or appointed to office therein, and to use our influence so that the governmental affairs of the city shall be conducted in an honest and economical manner, on a non-partizan basis, and purely on good business principles.

"To see that Grand Rapids is provided with the most approved and equitable system of taxation, the best-adapted system of street-paving, street-lighting, water-supply, of drainage and other sanitary precautions, of transit, of public schools, and all other public necessities and conveniences that promote the material and moral welfare of the city.

"It will be a special object of the League to make a thorough study and scientific investigation of the correct principles of local self-government, as adapted to this municipality, and to publish appropriate information on the defects and needs of our city government. Also, to use our influence for the proper amendment of our city charter, when required."

The executive committee consists of three, who meet once each month. The administration is divided among the following departments:

1. Municipal Reform Literature.
2. Public Schools.
3. City Water-supply.
4. City Drainage and Public Health.
5. Street-paving and Improvements.
6. City Taxation.
7. Ways and Means.
8. Public Street-lighting.
9. Compulsory Voting.
10. Rapid Public Transit.
11. Charter Amendments.
12. Public Morality.
13. Local Self-government.

The League is not restricted in its political action, and women are eligible to membership. The origin of the organization was the need for some kind of concerted and persistent effort which might result in the election of better men to the City Council, so that city affairs—the business of the city —might be conducted on business principles. In one respect the League was very wise in forming its board of managers from representative organizations in the city, such as the Real-estate Board, Central Labor Union, Builders' and Traders' Exchange, Building-trades Council, Retail Grocers' Association, Furniture Manufacturers' Association, Ministers' Conference, Charity Organization Society, Clearing-house Association, Young Men's Christian Association, Board of Education, Common Council, Press Association.

THE MUNICIPAL LEAGUE OF MILWAUKEE

President,
JOHN R. BUTLER.

Secretary,
EDWARD K. WEST,
2630 Wells Street,
Milwaukee, Wis.

The League was organized in March, 1893, but is not yet incorporated. A voluntary secretary directs the work. The annual membership fee is $1. There is no organ of the society, and as an association no active part is taken in politics.

"This organization is non-partizan, and seeks primarily to eliminate from the city and county governments every trace of national and State politics, and to introduce improved business principles and methods in the management of their affairs. It is not organized for spasmodic or sensational work as a campaign club, but for the purpose of maturing and suggesting for public consideration, from time to time, such reformatory measures in legislation and expenditures as the better sentiment of the community may approve.

"It is our intention to avoid all animosities, and primarily to address ourselves to the correction of the fundamental conditions of which imperfect government is the result. Nevertheless we mean to protest in unmistakable terms against existing evils, wherever it is believed that such a course will be beneficial, and where we think the public good requires it."

Women are not eligible to membership. An executive committee of seven meets once a month, subdividing the work into the following departments:

1. Laws and Legislation.
2. Press Relations.
3. Finance.
4. Special Inquiry.

The organization was the evidence of the existence of a strong sentiment throughout the city in favor of non-partizan municipal government and business administration of affairs. Those who have given time and best efforts gratuitously for the public good, as it is and as it is apprehended, will not be discouraged, but will continue their efforts. In reply to the question what results were actually accomplished, it was stated that it was difficult to prove direct results due to the League, but the three political parties adopted civil-service extension resolutions at the last spring (1894) conventions, and the character of men selected to represent the various wards in the Common Council was apparently greatly improved. This fact was due to agitation and personal efforts of members in their home wards. The League also made use of "heckling," of which this circular is an illustration:

MILWAUKEE, March 20, 1894.

"DEAR SIR: You having become a candidate for the suffrage of the people, the electors are entitled to your views on the leading questions involved in the present municipal election. We therefore submit to you two inquiries, and respectfully request your answer thereto.

"Will you kindly favor us with a short and explicit reply *on or before the 26th inst.*, as a mass-meeting of the League and friends of municipal reform has been called for the middle of the week, in order to consider the report and recommendations of the Committee on Political Agitation.

"Respectfully,
"JOHN A. BUTLER,
"*President.*

"EDWARD K. WEST,
"*Secretary.*"

THE MUNICIPAL LEAGUE OF OMAHA

President,
JUDGE G. W. DOANE.

Secretary,
GREGORY J. POWELL,
30th and Ohio Streets,
Omaha, Neb.

The League is not incorporated, but was organized May 29, 1894, with a voluntary secretary. Voluntary subscriptions support the society. An executive committee, meeting at the call of the chairman, superintends the following departments of work:

1. Municipal.
2. Philanthropic.
3. Industrial.
4. Educational.
5. Moral.

There is no organ of the League. Its lowest unit of organization is the ward. Not being restricted in its political action, it urges the nomination of good men, and if good candidates are not put up it will nominate independently. The League originated in a ministers' meeting, and by means of the interest aroused in municipal affairs laymen were invited to become members. In the constitution it is stated that "the object of this League shall be to quicken among its members and the citizens of Omaha an appreciation of their municipal obligations; to acquaint them with existing conditions; to familiarize them with the machinery of municipal government; to make conspicuous the respects in which such government is languidly or wrongly administered; to regard with jealous concern the point at which private interest enters into competition with the general good; and in every way to repress in the community what works to its detriment, and to foster whatsoever is calculated to promote its advantage.

"The principal means to be employed by the League are investigation, publication, agitation, and organization, together with the exercise of every moral influence needed to carry into effect the purposes of the League."

Results actually accomplished are the organization of local Leagues in four wards. The following statement of the objects of the League was printed on pledge-cards sent out to the citizens:

"1. To secure the best possible municipal government for Omaha.

"2. To attain this worthy object the League asks the coöperation of all citizens, irrespective of party or sect.

"3. It will be the purpose of the League to stimulate and secure the participation of every good citizen in municipal affairs.

"4. To emphasize the absolute necessity of electing only capable and honest men to fill all city offices, and placing this above every other consideration.

"5. We will urge every voter interested in the welfare of Omaha to take part in his own party primary and see that only candidates of such character are nominated.

"6. It will be a special object of the Municipal League to make a thorough investigation of local self-government as adapted to Omaha, and to collect and publish all appropriate information on the defects and needs of our city government, and do all in our power for the remedy and supply of the same."

THE MUNICIPAL LEAGUE OF PHILADELPHIA

President,
    GEORGE BURNHAM, JR.

Secretary,
    CLINTON ROGERS WOODRUFF,
        514 Walnut Street,
            Philadelphia, Pa.

The League is not yet incorporated, but was organized in the autumn of 1892. The secretary holds a salaried position.

According to its constitution, "the objects of the League shall be to eliminate all national and State politics from our municipal politics; to secure the nomination and election of candidates solely on account of their honesty and fitness for the office; to see that our municipal government be conducted upon non-partizan and strictly business principles; and to encourage every wise project for adding to the comfort and convenience of our citizens and to the prosperity and development of our city."

The League is supported by voluntary subscriptions. An executive committee of seven meets at the call of the chairman. There is no organ of the society. The unit of organization is in the election divisions of the city. There are standing committees on:

1. Executive.
2. Ward Organization.
3. Publication.
4. Current Legislation.
5. Foreign Population.
6. Naturalization.

THE MUNICIPAL LEAGUE

President,
A. P. STRONG.

Secretary,
C. B. MARTIN,
16 Gillespie Street,
Schenectady, N. Y.

The League was organized in 1894, but is not yet incorporated. The secretary holds a voluntary position. Financial support is secured by an annual membership fee of $1. The executive committee consists of seven members, who meet once a week. The standing committees are:

1. Public Library.
2. Municipal Legislation.
3. Good Order.
4. Public Health.
5. Education.
6. Publication.

There is no organ of the League, but it comes in touch with the workers through the various standing committees. Acceptance of a nomination to a municipal office is deemed a resignation of membership in the League. Women are not eligible to membership. There are no branches of the League in the municipal divisions. Increased sanitary precautions, prevention of unjust taxation, and an awakened public spirit are results already secured.

The Municipal League had its origin in the murder of Robert Ross. This event brought prominently to view the low level to which municipal affairs could descend when neglected by the best citizens, and led to a resolve to enlist as many citizens as possible in a more active interest in the city government. About one hundred of the leading citizens joined the movement. As the League has been in existence so short a time the membership is small, but the knowledge of its existence has had the effect of crystallizing the moral support of the best citizens. The League is non-partizan, but will expect the elected officials, from whatever party they may come, to do their duty; it will make suggestions to them, coöperate, or criticize, as may be deemed best. From the members of the League will be expected the full performance of their civic duties.

MUNICIPAL REFORM CLUB

President,
JOHN DUNN, JR.

Secretary,
G. H. STILWELL,
2 Clinton Block,
Syracuse, N. Y.

This Club was organized May 14, 1894, but is not yet incorporated. Membership fees of $1 per annum and contributions support the organization. The position of the secretary is voluntary. The executive committee of five meets at the call of the chairman. There is no organ of the society. Women are ineligible to membership. Political action is restricted to municipal affairs. According to its constitution, "the purposes of this organization shall be to secure the nomination and election of proper candidates for municipal offices, and the selection of fitting persons for appointive positions; to procure the punishment of any persons who may attempt frauds directly or indirectly affecting elections, or who may be guilty of maladministration of office, or misappropriation of public funds; to advocate and promote a public service based upon character and capacity only; and to promote intelligent discussion of municipal affairs by the collection, publication, and distribution of reliable information in relation thereto."

Regarding results actually accomplished the secretary writes:
"We have been represented a number of times before the Constitutional Convention, and are now working hard in favor of the amendments. We have helped organize clubs in Oswego and Rochester with similar aims. Our Club was formed on short notice in 1894, as the result of a letter to the chairman of the executive committee from Mr. Pryor, secretary of the City Club of New York, inquiring for some organization to help bring pressure on Governor Flower to get him to sign some of the New York City bills then pending. It was too late for that, but a paper read at a church meeting which dealt with these matters excited so much interest that we held a public meeting, at which some three hundred people were present, and speakers from New York and Buffalo; and about forty people signed a petition for the organization of such a club. We sent delegations to the State and National Municipal Leagues. We have done something toward subordinate local organization and membership, but the constitutional work took so much time that we have not done so much at home as we might have. We are just preparing for a winter cam-

paign preparatory to our local election in February. This, however, is somewhat disorganized again by a sudden call to Europe which falls on me, who have had the management of the affair as chairman of the executive committee. I hope very much that the constitutional amendments will pass. This will postpone our election till next fall and give time for a more complete ward organization. We are trying to affiliate with the Young People's Society of Christian Endeavor and all other societies looking in the same direction, except the American Protective Association. We have several prominent Roman Catholics among our supporters, and hope for more."

THE MUNICIPAL LEAGUE OF BOSTON

President,
SAMUEL B. CAPEN.

Secretary,
EDWIN D. MEAD,
20 Beacon Street,
Boston, Mass.

The date of the permanent organization was February 21, 1894, but the League is not yet incorporated. A voluntary secretary directs the work. The financial support is obtained from an annual assessment on the members. According to the constitution, "the objects of this League shall be to keep before our citizens the necessity of their interest in public affairs; to discuss and shape public opinion upon all questions which relate to the proper government of our city; to separate municipal politics from State and national politics; to secure the nomination and election of municipal officers solely on account of their fitness for the office; to federate for these purposes the various moral forces of the city; and to encourage every wise project for the promotion of the good order, prosperity, and honor of Boston."

All classes are members, but the preference is given to members of religious, civic, philanthropic, business, and labor organizations. The executive committee of seven holds meetings each month from October to April. The society has no organ of its own, but the work is divided among these departments:

1. Municipal Charter.
2. Ward Leagues.
3. Proportional Representation.
4. Candidates and Election.
5. Current Affairs and Municipal Legislation.
6. City Finance and Accounts.
7. Public Schools.
8. Public Health and Safety.
9. Public Work.
10. Charities and Correction.
11. Publication.

The extension of the League is contemplated by the organization of branches in each ward. Monthly public League meetings keep its objects before the community. Women are not eligible to membership. The president writes: "We are too young to speak of results, but we have certainly awakened all over the city renewed interest in municipal matters."

The League had its origin in an address made before the Congregational Club of Boston in March, 1892, which led at once to the formation of the Pilgrim Association of Boston, an organization of Congregationalists. That organization instructed its president to communicate with other similar religious, civic, and philanthropic societies, and ask for a federation of the moral forces of the city. The League now has a membership of about one hundred and fifty, and is limited to two hundred. At present it is putting especial effort into a movement to secure from the next State legislature important changes in the city charter, and also some plan of proportional representation.

NATIONAL CIVIL-SERVICE REFORM LEAGUE

President,
CARL SCHURZ.

Secretary,
GEORGE MCANENY,
54 William Street,
New York.

This League was organized in August, 1881, but is not incorporated. The League is composed of all the Civil-service Reform Associations in the United States, of which there are now thirty-two. It is supported by voluntary contributions. The secretary is also the secretary of the Civil-service Reform Association of New York City, and as such is a salaried officer. An executive committee of twenty-one manages the affairs of the League during the interim between its annual meetings, and meets subject to the call of the president. The standing committees are:

1. Publication Committee, to which is intrusted the control of the organ of the League, *Good Government.*
2. Finance Committee.

There are also committees, practically permanent, upon:

1. Reform in the Consular Service.
2. Selection of First, Second, and Third Class Postmasters.
3. Political Assessments.

Good Government, the organ of the League, published monthly at Washington and New York, forms a medium of communication as well as correspondence, and reports relative to the personal work of the officers and the local Leagues.

Political action is restricted, in that the League as such cannot advocate any party or candidate. Women are eligible to membership through some of the organizations.

The League was organized in order to keep the several Civil-service Reform Associations in touch with one another and unify their action. It is not greatly larger than it has been for some years, excepting through the recent organization of the Anti-spoils League, formed in December, 1893, now numbering about ten thousand members. The object of the League is to promote the merit system of appointment to administrative offices, to the end that such offices shall be filled, excepting so far as they are directly concerned with the policy of administration, on grounds of fitness, and not because of the personal or partizan relations of those seeking them.

The object of the League has been partially accomplished by the passage by Congress of the existing civil-service law and the gradual extension of its application to fifty thousand employees of the government, the adoption of State civil-service acts, applying also to all municipalities in Massachusetts and New York, and the adoption of civil-service rules by a number of single cities in other States.

NATIONAL MUNICIPAL LEAGUE

President,
JAMES C. CARTER.

Secretary,
CLINTON ROGERS WOODRUFF,
514 Walnut Street,
Philadelphia, Pa.

The National Municipal Reform League is a result of the National Conference for Good City Government, held in Philadelphia in the month of January, 1894. This conference brought together, from all parts of the country, men and women who had long given special thought to the government of our large cities; and its discussions showed clearly that the many and serious defects recognized in American municipal institutions are practically the same throughout the country, and arise from permanent and universal, not from temporary or local, causes. Complaints vary in form or degree, illustrations of imperfect working in the machinery of administration are diverse, but the general situation is substantially identical in all the great cities of the Union.

The National Municipal League was organized at the second conference, held in April, 1894, in the city of New York. The League affords counsel and encouragement to all its affiliated societies; it in no wise controls their action, for it recognizes the probability of honest and reasonable difference of opinion among its members regarding the most effective means to advance their common ends. If its true character and purposes are understood its utility must be apparent to every one in sympathy with those purposes. It aims to embrace all associations of citizens formed to improve municipal government; if such associations exist for yet other laudable ends, or to advocate some one special measure of reform in city administration, they are none the less eligible for affiliation. It brings together, at frequent intervals, for coöperation, instruction, and advice, accredited representatives from all such societies; but their action when assembled binds even the societies sending them so far only as it may merit the deliberate approval of their respective governing bodies.

According to its constitution, the League has a threefold object:

"1. To multiply the numbers, harmonize the methods, and combine the forces of all who realize that it is only by united action and organization that good citizens can secure the adoption of good laws and the selection of men of trained ability and proved integrity for all municipal positions, or prevent the success of incompetent or corrupt candidates for public office.

"2. To promote the thorough investigation and discussion of the conditions and details of civic administration, and of the methods for selecting and appointing officials in American cities, and of laws and ordinances relating to such subjects.

"3. To provide for such meetings and conferences, and for

the preparation and circulation of such addresses and other literature, as may seem likely to advance the cause of good city government."

The League is managed by a Board of Delegates chosen by the associations composing it. Each association is entitled to appoint, from time to time, as many delegates as it may see fit, and each delegate shall retain his position until he is withdrawn, or his successor is qualified, or his association becomes inactive.

The annual fee for associate members is $5. The League has no organ of its own, but from time to time issues leaflets on some topic connected with good government. The position of the secretary is voluntary. The executive committee consists of twelve, meeting at the call of the chairman. The departments of the League are:

1. Grievances and Abuses.   2. Law.   3. Publication.

THE REFORM LEAGUE

President,
JOSEPH PACKARD, JR.

Secretary,
CHARLES MORRIS HOWARD,
Equitable Building,
Baltimore, Md.

The date of organization was November, 1885, but the League has not been incorporated. The position of the secretary is voluntary. An annual fee of $1 from members and voluntary subscriptions furnish the financial support. An executive committee of fifteen, subject to the call of the chairman or of the president, meets about once each month. The departments of work are:

1. Finance.   4. Public Officials.
2. Legislation.   5. Publications.
3. Elections.   6. Membership.

At the April meeting, 1894, the following resolution was adopted by the League:

"*Resolved*, That the president appoint, as soon as practicable, the following permanent committees of the League, consisting of not less than five members each, each with the power to add to its number, with the consent of the president:

"1. A Committee upon the Opening, Closing, Making, Repairing, and Maintaining the Streets, Alleys, Sewers, Conduits, etc., of the City of Baltimore.

"2. A Committee upon the Preservation of the Health of the City of Baltimore and upon the Management of the City Institutions for the Care of the Sick and Infirm.

"3. A Committee upon the Cleaning and Lighting of the Public Streets and Alleys in the City of Baltimore.

"4. A Committee upon the Public Schools of the City of Baltimore.

"5. A Committee upon the Levy and Assessment of Taxes in the City of Baltimore.

"6. A Committee upon the Finances of the City of Baltimore.

"It shall be the duty of these various committees to acquaint themselves with the most approved methods of municipal work and the methods in use in this city, and in all ways to promote economy and efficiency in such work and the administration thereof. To this end they shall endeavor to secure the coöperation of the appropriate municipal departments as far as practicable. Each of these committees shall meet whenever called by the president of the League or their respective chairmen, who shall be named by the president, and shall each make at least one report annually to the League, and such special reports to the League or executive committee as each committee or the executive committee deems necessary."

The League has no organ of its own, and plans to come in touch with its members by means of reform clubs organized in each ward. Women are ineligible to membership. The political action of the League is unrestricted, because it "shall nominate or indorse all candidates for elective public offices to be supported by the League (unless the League shall in any case direct otherwise), and shall discharge any other duties which may be delegated to it by the League or the executive committee."

The object of the organization, as stated in its constitution, "shall be to secure fair elections, promote honest and efficient government, and to expose and bring to punishment official misconduct in the State of Maryland and especially in the city of Baltimore. It will adopt all legitimate and honorable means to effect these ends, and will strive to organize affiliated associations with analogous aims in the various counties of the State."

It has actually accomplished some of these results by securing better election and registration laws (including the Australian ballot), the conviction of fraudulent election officers, and somewhat fairer elections.

Ever since the election of 1875 in Baltimore City, which was a grossly fraudulent one, the general confidence in the fairness of elections there has become gradually impaired. In times of most active contest, of course, the frauds were grosser and more numerous. Such a campaign was the municipal election in November, 1885. At this election the mayoralty was the chief point of contention. The Independent Democrats nominated for this position a lifelong Democrat of unimpeachable standing, and he received the indorsement of the Republican party. The Democratic machine nominated a gentleman of personally decent character, but an outspoken advocate of machine men and methods. On the face of the returns the "regular" candidate was shown to have been elected by an insignificant majority. The frauds perpetrated at this election at the instance of the machine, and shortly afterward proved and published, were much more than sufficient to counterbalance the apparent majority. Several of the registers and election judges were convicted and imprisoned for their part in the frauds.

Just after this election the Reform League was formed, "to secure fair elections, promote honest government, and to expose and bring to punishment official misconduct in the State of Maryland and especially in the city of Baltimore." The constitution almost as it now stands was adopted; the by-laws have received considerable modification. Mr. S. Teackle Wallis was chosen president, and continued to occupy that position until his death, in April, 1894. Until lately no organized effort has been made since the formation of the League to increase its membership, which was at the outset about two hundred and fifty or three hundred. A Committee on Membership had been provided for in the by-laws, but had become inactive. Lately this committee has been reorganized, and as a result of its activity the League has about four hundred and fifty members, while new ones are coming in rapidly.

Last winter there were so many new evidences of the continued dominance of corrupt ring rule that the members of the League felt the necessity for arousing it to renewed activity. All the League's committees were reconstituted so as to get rid of inactive members, and the lists were filled by putting in energetic and, in most cases, younger men. At this time it was decided to widen the scope of the League from the investigation of election frauds and official dishonesty, toward which its efforts had been mainly directed, and to include the examination of municipal methods from the point of view of efficiency, without regard to the question of actual corruption. With this end in view the constitution, which had previously aimed at promoting "honest government," was amended so as to read "promote honest and efficient government." At the same time, and with the same object, the additional special permanent committees to investigate the work of certain city departments were created. It is hoped, if this work is found successful, that it may lead to the appointment of similar permanent committees to supervise the work of all the leading departments, and may prevent or check many abuses by giving them publicity.

THE SOCIAL REFORM CLUB

President,
    ERNEST H. CROSBY.

Secretary,
    JOHN N. BOGERT,
    7 Lafayette Place,
    New York.

This Club was organized November 26, 1894, with a secretary serving voluntarily. "A deep interest in social reform, and especially in the elevation of society by the improvement of the condition of wage-workers, shall be the indispensable qualification of membership in this Club." The membership shall consist, as far as possible, in equal proportions of wage-workers and of others possessing the above-mentioned qualification. The membership dues are $1 a year. According to its constitution the objects of the Club are:

"1. To form a common center at which wage-earners and others interested in the labor movement may meet to consider the next step or steps which should be taken in order to improve industrial and social conditions in the city of New York.

"2. The specific characteristic of this Club is to be that it shall take no share in the propaganda of general theories of society, and shall rigidly exclude all so-called 'social panaceas' from its discussions, but shall confine itself to the consideration, the advocacy, and the carrying out of practical measures such as can be undertaken in the immediate future with fair hope of success, and commend themselves to conscience and to common sense."

There are five standing committees of the club, to which others may be added as occasion may require. These are:

1. Membership.
2. Legislation.
3. Application of the Law.
4. Enforcement of the Law.
5. Instruction.

Its directing body is an executive council of fifteen members, which appoints the five standing committees. The executive council is also bound, "in the case of all extensive strikes and lockouts, to do its utmost to promote conciliation and arbitration; and, in case these methods should fail, to investigate the merits of the question or questions at issue, and, after due and impartial consideration, to use the influence of the Club, and, when necessary, the funds at its command, in favor of that party on whose side justice shall be found."

As this Club has been organized so recently no reports of actual progress can yet be made.

SOCIETY FOR THE PREVENTION OF CRIME

President,
   CHARLES H. PARKHURST.

Secretary,
   THADDEUS D. KENNESON,
      11 William Street,
      New York.

The Society was organized October 22, 1878, and incorporated October 30, 1878. The secretary's position is voluntary, and the constitution expressly provides that all positions in the Society shall be voluntary. Voluntary subscriptions support the Society's work. Three comprise the executive committee, which meets once a week. There are two standing committees:

1. Executive.
2. Finance.

The Society is restricted in its political action. According to its certificate of incorporation, its objects are: "To promote in all proper and suitable ways the removal of sources and causes of crime; to assist the weak and helpless in obtaining the protection of the courts and of the laws regulating the sale of intoxicating drinks, and in protecting themselves against the temptations to crime; to aid in the enforcement of the laws of this State; to disseminate information, and to arouse a correct public opinion in support of all laws, organizing and forming meetings and associations for instruction and discussion upon such topics."

The Society is a close corporation with a very small membership. The members elect officers and directors; the directors appoint an executive committee, which manages details and reports monthly to the directors. The executive committee employs a superintendent and various agents, whom it directs from week to week. The present executive committee is the president, the secretary, and Frank Moss, who acts as voluntary counsel. There is no rule of the Society which makes women ineligible to membership, but there are no female members at the present time. The great result achieved by the Society for the Prevention of Crime was the exposure of the corruption in the police department. This was secured by means of the Lexow Investigating Committee. The forces thus set in motion were powerful factors in the overthrow of Tammany Hall in the November election of 1894.

The Society, under the presidency of Rev. Howard Crosby, D.D., LL.D., did very effective work in the line of its corporate purpose, and especially in stimulating public sentiment and in securing good legislation and defeating bad measures in matters touching crime. In its work the collusion between criminals and the officers of the law became apparent, and its efforts were then directed against official complicity with crime. This latter phase of work became more marked under the administration of the present president, and has just reached a successful period, gratifying alike to the members of the Society and to the citizens of the city and State.

THE TRADES LEAGUE OF PHILADELPHIA

President,
W. W. FOULKROD.

Secretary,
J. N. FITZGERALD,
421 Chestnut Street,
Philadelphia, Pa.

The date of organization was March 24, 1891, and of incorporation, June, 1894. A salaried secretary has the general oversight. The annual dues are $10. According to the constitution, "the Trades League is organized for the purpose of improving the commerce, the business, and the manufacturing interests of the port and city of Philadelphia; to advocate and encourage any and all measures that tend to benefit the business, the prosperity, or the convenience of the citizens of Philadelphia."

An executive committee of forty meets once each month, and the standing committees are the following:

1. Passenger Transportation.
2. Freight Transportation.
3. Membership.
4. Entertainment.
5. Finance.
6. Harbor and Navigation.
7. Legislation.
8. Improvement and Interests of Philadelphia.
9. Press.
10. Municipal Affairs.
11. Law.

The society has no organ of its own, but comes in touch with the workers by means of meetings and lunches. There is no venturing on political questions, except in connection with some substantial business question, and only when it cannot be avoided. Women are ineligible to membership.

"The meeting for the organization of the Trades League

was held in answer to a public call, in which the business men of our city realized the necessity of organizing in order to devise plans by which our city might be put on an equal footing with other cities of her class, and to endeavor to accomplish by organization that which seemed impossible to be done by individuals.

"That the Trades League has accomplished considerable there can be no question of doubt, and that there is yet much to be accomplished none of us can deny; but we have made a good start, and the future will depend largely upon the support you give us.

"The fact that there is such an organization in Philadelphia, watching and at all times ready to take up and endeavor to remove any obstacle that is injurious to our business interests, and, at the same time, prevent new ones being thrust upon us, must of itself have a beneficial effect upon our business."

Among the list of actual accomplishments of the League the larger number concern special interests, but others affect the community. The secretary writes:

"In reply to your note requesting six of the most important results achieved by the Trades League, would state that so many matters of importance have been successfully handled by our organization that it becomes somewhat difficult to reply. However, would state that the following advantages for the welfare of Philadelphia have been achieved by our organization:

"1. The stop-over privilege for Philadelphia on all through Eastern tickets *via* our city without extra charge.

"2. The establishment of a Freight Bureau under the charge of an efficient manager.

"3. Have been successful in inducing our city to refuse to grant to the Bell Telephone Company any more privileges without receiving something in return, one demand being that the company fix a low maximum rate for service.

"4. The settlement of the Mint site question, thus securing the Mint for Philadelphia.

"5. The publication of the 'Book of Philadelphia,' a highly artistic and illustrated publication designed to place before the country at large Philadelphia's superior advantages as a place of manufacturing, business, and commercial operations, and as a place of residence.

"6. The free distribution of Philadelphia newspapers in the principal hotels of leading cities throughout the world."

III

MOVEMENTS FOR CIVIC BETTERMENT

I believe that the safety of our American institutions lies in the clear and honest appreciation on the part of each man that he has a right to stand up on his own feet; that he has a right to his own opinion, and that he has a right to express it. And I believe that one great object toward which we have to labor is the building up of that appreciation in the minds and hearts of each growing young man. Now just observe the relation in which the boss stands to that idea. There is a broad line to be drawn between a leader and a boss. There always will be a leader. The leader is he who has the power of reproducing his own conceptions, his own ideas, in the minds of those that are in any way subordinated to his influence. In other words, the office of the leader is to make more and more of the men that are brought under his influence; the object of the boss is to make less and less of the men that are brought under his influence. The boss is the most sagaciously devised scheme that has yet been originated for the purpose of crushing out, weakening, and drying up individual personality; and therefore you and I, young friends, to our dying gasp, are going to fight the boss, whatever may be his professions of respectability. The more respectable he is, the more damnably dangerous he is.

C. H. PARKHURST.

III

MOVEMENTS FOR CIVIC BETTERMENT

The movements thus far described have concerned themselves with municipal reform in the narrower sense; but there are many other movements which are making for civic betterment—that is, the improvement of the municipality in any of the thousand ways in which this may be accomplished. Municipal reform at once conveys the idea that a great amount of destructive work is involved; that there must be an immense tearing down, in order that the ground may be cleared for improved conditions. In a great many cases that fact is true, as, for example, in New York there could be no true reform till Tammany Hall and all which that organization stood for was utterly destroyed. Now that the overthrow of that organization is a fact, the work of reform must henceforth be devoted to the keenest vigilance that there shall be no further necessity for the destructive work, and that there shall be ample provision for the constructive or the positive program. It is not enough that the streets of the city be kept scrupulously clean and the tax-rate kept at the lowest notch—in other words, that the claims of property be given the precedence over those of life; but there is a need for a greater expenditure of the city's money, in order that provision may be made for the suitable satisfaction of all the rational demands of all the elements in the make-up of the city. To illustrate: the mayor of St. Louis writes, under date of November 2, 1894: "St. Louis has no public lavatories on the streets, nor elsewhere, except in the parks, where the commissioner provides them." The park commissioner writes, under the same date, that there is a surface of 1732 acres in their parks, and that there are twenty-four lavatories. Why should New York be without municipal lodging-houses, public baths and wash-houses, open spaces, small parks, and markets, in a word, municipal provision for the needs and even comforts of all the component parts of a great city, but particularly the control by the municipality of those characteristics necessary to the continuance of the city, such, for example, as means of transportation, the water supply, gas and electric lighting, education, especially the departments of art, technical and manual training? There are therefore organized movements that are working along these lines, and are demanding that there shall be provision for these positive features. This chapter will be devoted to a summary of what such organizations are striving to accomplish for their own particular localities, because the cause of civic betterment will be greatly indebted to them.

Some of these societies are distinctively new, or are using entirely new methods in dealing with the problems of the day. Thus the university or the social settlement illustrates a new phase of humanitarian effort, while temperance work is carried on along the same general lines. Accordingly a knowledge of the work of the various temperance societies, labor organizations, Young Men's Christian Associations, the varied phases of educational institutions, and the spiritual efforts of the church will be assumed, while the following descriptions will concern movements which need to be more widely known by those who are concerned in the welfare of their municipality. Those who are interested in the object of their particular society are of necessity specialists, but a comprehensive survey of the entire field of work is of great value, because some other agency may be doing the same kind of work as the organization in question, but vastly better. How not to do it is one lesson which the philanthropy of 1895 is learning by bitter experience.

THE AMERICAN INSTITUTE OF CHRISTIAN SOCIOLOGY

President,
L. T. CHAMBERLAIN.

Secretary,
WILLIAM HOWE TOLMAN,
427 West Fifty-seventh Street,
New York.

In order to grapple with the vexed and vexing problems of the day the study of their causes and also of their theories is necessary. It is therefore the aim of the Institute to bring together those who are already interested in the study of the social problems, and to organize other groups for the same purpose. Organization is merely the first step, for the Institute will then furnish suggested topics for study, and will prepare outlines in order that the instruction may be definite and scientific. Richard T. Ely, who was the first president of the Institute, said of it: " Its purpose is twofold: first, to endeavor to ascertain the truth in regard to the social questions of the time; and, second, to endeavor to apply the truth practically. The Institute hopes directly and indirectly to promote the pursuit of knowledge and thus to add to the sum total of our knowledge, and it desires to bring our social life, as well as our individual life, into harmony with the teachings of Christ." According to its constitution, the objects of the Institute are the following:

" 1. To claim for the Christian law the ultimate authority to rule social practice.

" 2. To study in common how to apply the principles of Christianity to the social and economic difficulties of the present time.

"3. To present Christ as the living Master and King of men, and his kingdom as the complete ideal of human society, to be realized on earth."

There seems to be hungering and thirsting for civic righteousness on the part of the rising generation, and it will be the aim of the Institute to supply the requisite satisfaction. Sociology is claiming to be a science, and if that claim is established there is all the more need for a scientific study of the underlying principles. There are certain theories which seem very attractive to those whose attention has been called to the problems of society for the first time; but as they are studied, particularly in the light of comparative facts, they undergo considerable modification. If now the growing citizenship of the country is to be a power for good, it must be intelligent, so that it will not be led captive by the party or the party boss; it must also be as mindful of its duties as of its rights.

THE ALTRURIAN LEAGUE

Secretary,
W. J. GHENT,
53 East Tenth Street,
New York.

Among the newer organizations is this League, which was founded May 11, 1894. It is now entirely educational in its character, believing that before action can be wisely taken there must be a thorough knowledge of conditions, with all their various manifestations. The League originated among a small group of people—three of whom were members of the London Fabian Society—holding somewhat radical views on social reform, and feeling the urgency of getting together all others of similar beliefs, in order to propagate these beliefs among the masses. The League is not restricted in its political action, and women are eligible to membership. There are no standing committees, but as the need for particular work arises special committees are then appointed. An executive committee directs the work. The support of the society is obtained solely from its members, who are composed of those desirous of making a systematic inquiry into the applicability to American conditions of the principle of collective ownership of the means of production and distribution. The object of the League is, accordingly, the systematic study of economics, the determining a remedy for existing social wrongs, and the agitation for a correction of those evils.

BETTER DWELLINGS SOCIETY

Secretary,
ARTHUR B. ELLIS,
103 Milk Street,
Boston, Mass.

The increasing attention which is paid to all the problems of housing in our large cities is a proof of the great importance of the question. Whatever impairs the integrity of the home is to be deplored, for the home is one of the basic elements of a healthful municipal life. Those who have given even a superficial study to the evils of the tenement-house are aware how great a menace they are to a normal development, particularly of the life of the children. Poor citizens are the usual product of poor homes. The above Society, conscious of these facts, was organized to aid in improving the sanitary condition of Boston, and especially of its tenement-houses. The date of organization was May 5, 1892, some time after the following action:

ASSOCIATED CHARITIES OF BOSTON.
CENTRAL OFFICE, 41 CHARITY BUILDING.

The Board of Directors, December 11, 1891, adopted the following:

"In view of the growing interest and increase in public sensitiveness concerning the worst homes in which poor people are allowed to live, the board believes that now is the time for a vigorous effort to aid the Board of Health in causing such tenements either to be improved or vacated.

"The board will therefore take steps, through its Committee on Tenements, to invite representatives from the Boston Coöperative Building Company, the Improved Dwellings Association, the Working-men's Building Association, and the public at large, to form, with members of the Associated Charities, a joint committee, with power to add to their number, to take such action as they may deem fit to improve the tenements of the poorest of our population, or, where these tenements are so bad that they cannot be made habitable, to cause them to be vacated."

Robert Treat Paine is the president of the Society. As the principal object of the Society is the investigation of unfit tenements, all the resources are brought to bear on this and on allied topics. A valuable report was made on the alley tenements, and a memorial presented to the city authorities requesting them to take the proper measures to improve existing conditions. A report was also published showing the conditions of private ways. The work of the Society is greatly promoted by women, who are eligible to membership.

THE BROTHERHOOD OF THE KINGDOM

Secretary,
REV. SAMUEL ZANE BATTEN,
312 West Fifty-fourth Street,
New York.

Within the past few years there has been a wonderful revival of the civic and more especially of the religious sense of obligation toward the municipality. The foremost reformer of our times is a Christian minister, and the issue in his magnificent campaign was solely that between right and wrong. He held that his religious sphere of action was circumscribed unless it included a conscious effort to make his city better. This awakened sense of civic obligation has crystallized into various organizations in the churches, and any summary of the factors entering into municipal betterment would be incomplete without them. The aim of the above organization must serve as a type of the various efforts which are being made by church-members, of whatever creed, to make communities, especially the cities, centers of true and permanent happiness. Some of the brotherhoods are organized more distinctively for spiritual development and extension, but in so far as they rest content with that object they will not fulfil their full measure of usefulness.

The Brotherhood of the Kingdom was the outcome of weekly meetings of two men, who appreciated the great advantage of conference and discussion of social topics. With the idea of increasing its sphere of action, one more brother was included. The membership became so large, that in 1894 a summer conference of three days was held at Marlborough-on-Hudson. One of the days was devoted to a discussion of social topics, such as the land question, while at the evening session the theme was that of municipal reformation. One of the two men, Walter Rauschenbusch, has been identified with the Brotherhood so long that he is the best suited to set forth its aim and scope; hence his statement is authoritative:

"The Brotherhood of the Kingdom was founded upon the conviction that the great aim of Christ was the establishment of the kingdom of God, and that this should be the aim of the church and of every Christian. It believes that this aim has been largely forgotten, misunderstood, or curtailed by the Christian church, and the Brotherhood was formed 'to reestablish this idea in the thought of the church and to assist in its practical realization in the world.'

"Looking only for their own salvation, Christian men have

often forgotten the unsaved world; seeking exclusively for the salvation of individual souls, they have not striven as they might to permeate the collective life of humanity, in politics, industry, science, and art, with the spirit of Christ; hoping for perfection only in a future life, they have too easily surrendered this life to selfishness. Hence the double standard of morality for private and business life which is prevalent among us. Hence the difficulty of getting the stored-up moral and religious energies of the Christian community to bear on civic life. The Brotherhood would inscribe on the banner of Christianity a word large enough to embrace the whole of life, inside and outside, religious and industrial, individual and social; and no word is great enough except the tremendous word of the Jewish prophets and of Jesus Christ—'the kingdom of God.'

"The Brotherhood believes profoundly in the unexhausted power of Christianity. Christianity saves individuals: it can save cities and nations, if once its forces are exerted in that direction. No other force has yet appeared in history which is able to regenerate life, and that without the religious factor all social effort is doomed to be spasmodic and futile.

"The Brotherhood seeks to accomplish its aims by encouraging its members to obedience to the ethics of Jesus; by exemplifying Christian fellowship and community of interests among its members; by propagating the thoughts of Jesus by correspondence, speech, and press; by turning the attention of religious men to social work, and by infusing the religious spirit into social workers; and by lending a hand unselfishly to every honest effort to increase the sum total of righteousness, truth, and mercy among men."

Such is what might be called the ideal of the Brotherhood; but it is not merely an ideal, for its principles have been translated into actual workaday effort. Thus several of its members have been active in arranging for the celebrated Municipal Program Conferences. Others have lent their influence to the Working-women's Society in its efforts for the store "salesladies." One drew up a bill for State employment bureaus and advocated it before a committee of the legislature of New York; another did similar work in the legislature of New Jersey. Several have arranged for the making of programs for public meetings, and see to it that social topics are not neglected, but that live men are put on.

THE CHARITY ORGANIZATION SOCIETY OF THE CITY OF NEW YORK

President,
ROBERT W. DE FOREST.

Secretary,
CHARLES D. KELLOGG,
105 East Twenty-second Street,
New York.

The discussion which would omit any mention of the work of organized charity in the bettering of civic conditions is sadly deficient. The term "Charity Organization" does not denote a new scheme for dispensing charity, but describes the attempt to organize existing charities—to bring into harmony all the humane efforts of private benevolence, societies, institutions, or of municipal and State authorities.

The New York Society has been selected as a typical organization; and its methods, subject to what changes may be necessitated by local conditions, will give an accurate idea of the methods in other cities.

A salaried secretary directs the work, which is subdivided into various departments. The executive committee of nine meets bi-weekly. The organ of the Society is the monthly, the *Charities Review*. For its own use the Society divides the city into ten irregular districts. There is a sharp restriction as to political action. Women are eligible to membership.

In 1881 the State Board of Charities saw that an agency was needed in New York City to prevent the waste of charitable effort and the mischievous results of unwise and inexperienced distribution of alms. By the official action of that board this Society was inaugurated.

It was then estimated that there were in New York about 350 local charitable institutions, disbursing not less than $4,000,000 annually. The Commissioners of Charities and Correction were expending annually $1,500,000, and 490 religious bodies at least $375,000 more. Adding to these the thousands of householders and individuals daily responding to appeals for relief, the aggregate was computed at not less than $8,000,000. All these distinct agencies were to be brought, as far as possible, into such accord that their own efficiency should be enhanced, the woes of poverty mitigated, and the dangers of pauperism averted.

As stated in the constitution, its objects are:

" 1. To be a center of intercommunication between the various churches and charitable agencies in the city; to foster harmonious coöperation between them, and to check the evils of the overlapping of relief.

" 2. To investigate thoroughly, and without charge, the cases of all applicants for relief which are referred to the Society for inquiry, and to send the persons having a legitimate interest in such cases full reports of the results of investigation; to provide visitors, who shall personally attend cases needing counsel and advice.

" 3. To obtain from the proper charities and charitable individuals suitable and adequate relief for deserving cases.

" 4. To procure work for poor persons who are capable of being wholly or partially self-supporting.

" 5. To repress mendicity by the above means and by the prosecution of impostors.

" 6. To promote the general welfare of the poor by social and sanitary reforms and by the inculcation of habits of providence and self-dependence."

What the Society has actually accomplished is the accumulation of more or less information concerning upward of 200,000 families and persons (equivalent to at least 500,000 individuals) who have applied for or received relief. It deals with 7000 or 8000 cases of alleged destitution yearly, sends 4000 to 5000 reports to societies, churches, and private donors. It also maintains a laundry to employ and educate poor women; a Wayfarers' Lodge—a night refuge where homeless men are lodged, fed, and bathed, for which they give an equivalent in work; a wood-yard to test and aid men, chiefly the homeless; a Penny Provident Fund, to promote thrift and saving among the poor; and a workroom for unskilled women, to supply both training and employment to a limited extent.

THE INSTITUTIONAL CHURCH

	Pastor,
THE AMITY BAPTIST CHURCH,	REV. LEIGHTON WILLIAMS,
312 West Fifty-fourth Street,	305 West Eighty-eighth Street,
New York.	New York.

In recent years the above phrase has come into use, and designates what might be called the church at work, not only on the Sabbath and on the prayer-meeting night, but seven days in the week, and the greater part of the twenty-four hours in each day. The Amity Baptist Church has been selected as a typical organization.

During the last five years the pastor and people of Amity Church, recognizing the need of effort in the direction of civic betterment, have been engaged, both individually and collectively, in working toward that end, and in consequence have naturally and gradually extended the scope of their church-work, until now Amity Church is coming to be known as an "institutional church."

The aim of the church is twofold: (1) to secure the conversion of individuals and their building up in the Christian life; (2) to promote the development of a truly Christian society, and to extend the rule of Christ in all departments of social, industrial, and civic life.

To achieve these ends the methods of work are:

1. The church with its multiplied services.

2. The Bible and industrial schools and kindergarten, the latter meeting daily and numbering fifty-four children.

3. The societies connected with the church, viz., Missionary, Christian Endeavor, Young Men's and Young Women's, Boys' Brigade, and Working-men's Institute. The headquarters of the Brotherhood of the Kingdom and of the Working-women's Society are located also in Amity Building.

4. Medical and charitable work, viz., dispensary, clinic for ear and throat diseases, poor relief, employment bureau.

5. Amity Mission (on Eleventh Avenue), with its evening evangelistic services, working-girls' lunch, and mothers' meetings.

6. The Amity Missionary Conference, held on the first Monday in April and the two following days, and including Christians of all denominations. Annual reports of this conference are printed. It is now in its fifth year.

7. The Amity Municipal Program Conferences, now in their second year.

8. The Amity tracts and leaflets. These publications contain articles on religious, educational, industrial, and social topics, and have had a wide circulation; and hardly any one whose opinion carries weight, withholds his approval from the social and theological propaganda in which the pastor and people are engaged.

Amity Church has thus made its influence felt throughout the city and country, and is coming to be known as a center of living, earnest, and broad-minded activity.

In addition to the above-mentioned methods it is the intention of the church to engage in the training and support of deaconesses. With this object in view a society has been organized in conjunction with the Second German Baptist Church, Rev. Walter Rauschenbusch, pastor.

To more efficiently carry on this last-named work it is the desire of the church to erect a dormitory building, a counterpart of the Amity school-building, but four stories in height, capable of furnishing accommodation to a large force of deaconesses and other workers.

The home of this extensive and varied work is known as the Amity Building, 312 West Fifty-fourth Street, adjoining the church edifice, three stories in height, and containing two school-rooms; waiting-room, drug-room, and consulting-room for dispensary and clinic; young men's reading-room; toilet-rooms; janitor's rooms; large studio; and rooms for a church visitor. The building is free from debt.

IDEALS FOR AMITY CHURCH

"1. *The Field:* the ward or parish; the city; the nation; the world.

"To cultivate an intelligent interest in all these, founded on accurate knowledge. While cultivating a broad sympathy, world-wide in extent, to make the ward or parish the subject of immediate and thorough investigation, not only on its religious side, but in all its aspects, industrial and social as well.

"2. *Coöperation.*

"To cultivate the spirit of brotherly coöperation with all 'men of good-will,' of every creed, nationality, and political affiliation, in temperance, municipal reform, and every other good work, along such lines as are practicable without the compromise of any principle on either part.

"To do all work in conjunction with others wherever possible, and hence to foster all union societies.

" 3. *The Training and Maintenance of Workers.*

"To gradually gather together a large force of volunteer workers, viz., lay brothers and deaconesses, willing to give themselves to the service of others without compensation further than the assurance of food, clothing, and shelter, but without permanent vows.

"The cultivation of the *communal life* in this way, and the illustration in our time of its beauty and its power.

"The building up of this ideal through the *settlement* plan, both rural and civic, and by semi-annual and other conferences.

" 4. *The Union of the Religious and Industrial Forces in the Salvation of Mankind.*

"To this end to heal the breach now existing. Hence we have started the Christian Working-men's Institute, for lectures, conferences, and debates.

" 5. *The Education of the People, and especially the Workers, in Correct Social and Religious Principles.*

"To this end the oral instruction from pulpit and platform, the schools, kindergartens, and tract distribution."

MUNICIPAL LABOR BUREAUS[*]

The more recent disturbances between labor and capital clearly indicate that any maladjustment of the equilibrium of these two great forces is attended with disaster to society, particularly the wage-workers, who are the first to feel the effects of such a conflict. Strife is not a normal condition of a civic community; accordingly, whatever will tend to satisfy the legitimate demands of labor will to that extent minimize

---

[*] I am indebted to Mr. Mornay Williams for the details of this system. Mr. Williams has been very much interested in an attempt to introduce the system into New York State, and has appeared several times before the Assembly to advocate its adoption.

the friction and bring about harmonious working. The problem of the unemployed is one of pressing importance, because the industrial crisis of the last few years has demonstrated that the great cities have been unable to successfully grapple with this question. In the opinion of those who are the most capable of judging, the coming years will test to the utmost all those remedies and solutions which have been and will be suggested in order to cope with this question. While there is no *one* solution of the industrial or any of the other pressing problems of the day, there are certain elements of a solution which will greatly tend to minimize the evil effects of these questions. One of the elements in the attempt to bring about an harmonious working between labor and capital is the Municipal Labor Bureau.

The first bureau was organized in the United States in the State of Ohio, as the outgrowth of a recommendation made at the Municipal Labor Congress held in Cincinnati in 1889, the initiative toward the movement having been a report on the Free Public Intelligence Office of France. Such bureaus exist to-day in the cities of Cincinnati, Dayton, Toledo, Cleveland, and Columbus. Attempts have been made to introduce similar legislation in the States of Iowa, Minnesota, and New York, and a bill was introduced in the legislature of the State of New York at the last session—in the Senate by Senator O'Connor and in the House by Mr. Lawson; the bill, however, never reached the order of third reading.

In the British colony of New Zealand Municipal Labor Bureaus have proved very effective. The English labor-leader, Mr. John Burns, member of Parliament and of the London County Council, advocates the formation of such bureaus in all towns, and so far from believing that such action will militate against the rights of organized labor, states that in his opinion the labor bureaus will probably lead to the trades-unions leaving their present meeting-places in public-houses, and using, alternatively, the rooms of the bureau or, as is being done, of the town hall for their meetings. He also advocates the formation of the bureaus as one means of differentiation of the laborer from the loafer.

No organized movement for the formation of Municipal Labor Bureaus is known to the writer, but the commissioners of labor statistics generally throughout the States have recommended the movement, and the American Federation of Labor indorses it.

THE MUNICIPAL PROGRAM CONFERENCES

Secretary,
WILLIAM HOWE TOLMAN,
427 West Fifty-seventh Street,
New York.

Five men in New York felt that there was a great amount of overlapping and duplication in the various efforts that were being made for the betterment of the city. They had several meetings, and by common consent determined that they would try to bring together in conferences, for the discussion of common municipal interests, a thoughtful audience on the one hand and a number of men and women who were specialists, on the other. The promoters of these conferences represented no organization or society, but they determined that they would arrange such a program as would attract the attention of any one with even a smattering of civic pride, and that they would then invite the very best people in the city to take part in the conferences. With only one exception did any one who was asked to assist at the gatherings refuse—a fact that was indicative of the public spirit on the part of the men and women who were willing to present these topics to their fellow-citizens. Another element in the success of the meetings was the fact that so few were instrumental in arranging for them, as the committee was practically a unit in the general purpose of the series, with only a slight divergency of opinion as to the details. It has been the experience of the committee that a few men who understand one another and are practically agreed on a general policy can accomplish a great deal more than a larger body.

It was the object of these conferences to promote an intelligent interest in the subject of municipal government, and to provide an opportunity for the free and courteous discussion of current municipal topics, looking toward a line of action positive and constructive rather than negative and destructive; measures rather than men. The central thought of the first series was New York, and the general program was: The Need of a Positive Program; The New Social Spirit; New York's Workers, Dependents, Houses, Saloons, Amusements, Needs, Thoroughfares; New York for New-Yorkers; and New York's Political Prospects. Among those who consented to preside were Major-General Howard, Samuel Gompers, ex-Mayor Hewitt, R. W. Gilder, Mrs. Lozier, Dr. Parkhurst, and Carl Schurz. As illustrative of the catholicity of the conferences, at the one on New York's Political Prospects, at which members of the various parties were to tell what they proposed to do for the city, there were present representatives from Tammany Hall, the Democratic, the Republican, the People's, and the Socialist-Labor parties. These men met on a common platform and made a plea for their respective parties. At the conferences representatives from some of the city departments were invited to discuss topics relating to them. Thus the Hon. Charles F. McLean, the then Commissioner of Police, read a paper on the subject of "Municipal Lodging-houses." The failure on the part of the community to interest itself in its public servants is one reason for the laxity in some of the departments of a great city. If it were known by a public official that there is a body of intelligent citizens who are informing themselves regarding his official acts, the knowledge of that fact would act as a strong deterrent force from any contemplated irregularity, and at the same time serve as a wonderful stimulus to perform conscientiously the duties of the office in question. There is one organization in this city—the City Vigilance League—which is in the field with those particular objects in view.

The same general idea characterized the second set of conferences for 1894–95; hence the list of the subjects will sufficiently indicate their scope. Seven of the papers have been published, and it is the intention that others shall be published just as soon as the publication fund will admit. The conference subjects for 1895 are: The Positive Program Begun; The New Social Spirit; The People; The People's Schools; The People's Safety; The People's Homes; The People's Revenues; The People's Health; The People's Transportation; The People's Recreation; The People's Literature; The People's Workshops; The People's City.

All inquiries concerning the first set of conferences should be sent to the secretary of the conferences for 1894–95. A fee of $1 will entitle the sender to all the conference literature for the coming season, as well as the leaflets already issued. This material will be of the greatest value to those who may wish to initiate similar conferences in other parts of the country.

THE SOCIAL SETTLEMENT

Within the last decade applied Christianity has been manifesting itself in the university or social settlements. The settlement idea is the exponent of the neighborhood principle: that if you wish to exert an uplifting influence on a community it cannot be done at long range, but there must be the contactual relations. Accordingly, sets of men or groups of women have taken residence in those parts of the city which have been the last to feel any other influence than that of their own peculiar miserable or vicious surroundings. The first experiment in this direction was made by Oxford and Cambridge men, who took residence in London at Toynbee Hall, the alma mater of the university settlements. After the start had been made several other settlements were organized by college men and also by the graduates from the women's colleges.

As the type of the settlement idea, Hull House, of Chicago, has been selected, because this social settlement, as the founder calls it, most closely approximates the ideal. In the first place, the settlement is located in the center of an industrial district, South Halsted Street. As Miss Addams said:

"'The original residents came to Hull House with a conviction that social intercourse could best express the growing sense of the economic unity of society. They wished the social spirit to be the undercurrent of the life of Hull House, whatever direction the stream might take. All the details were left for the demands of the neighborhood to determine, and each department has grown from a discovery made through natural and reciprocal social relations."

A brief enumeration of the activities that center at the Hull House is the best illustration of its wide sphere of influence; but even then any attempted measure of its influence is most unsatisfactory, because the population is so shifting and the opportunities for permanent-influence are so exceedingly brief. The House is the home of the college extension courses for that locality. These courses do not attempt to duplicate the other educational facilities in the city, but they supplement them by emphasizing the humanities, and leave the bread-and-butter studies to the schools. A Students' Association, composed of the attendants at these classes, is divided into literary, dramatic, musical, and debating sections, which hold monthly meetings for the continuance of their special objects, thus keeping alive the social and friendly spirit that was evoked by the extension courses. A reading-room is made possible by the coöperation of the city public library. Picture exhibitions, Sunday concerts, singing-classes, and a choral society stimulate the recreative life of the locality.

What is known as the "Jane Club" is a practical demonstration of the successful working of a social theory. The Jane Club, a coöperative boarding-club for young working-women, had the advice and assistance of Hull House in its establishment. The original members of the club, seven in number, were a group of trades-union girls accustomed to organized and coöperative action. The club has been from the beginning self-governing, without a matron or outside control, the officers being elected by the members from their own number and serving for six months gratuitously. The two offices of treasurer and steward have required a generous sacrifice of their limited leisure, as well as a good deal of ability, from those holding them. This being given, together with a considerable *esprit de corps* in the increasing number of members, the club has thriven both substantially and socially. The weekly dues of $3, with an occasional small assessment, have met all current expenses of rent, service, food, heat, and light, after the furnishing and first month's rent was supplied by Hull House. The club now numbers fifty members, and the one flat is increased to five. The members do such share of the housework as does not interfere with their daily occupations. There are various circles within the club for social and intellectual purposes, and while the members are glad to procure the comforts of life at a rate within their means, the atmosphere of the club is one of comradeship rather than thrift. The club holds a monthly reception in the Hull House gymnasium.

The Coffee-house and Kitchen is now a permanent element in the communal life of the settlement. The room itself is an attractive copy of an English inn, with low, dark rafters, diamond windows, and large fireplace. It is open every day from six in the morning to eleven at night. An effort has been made to combine the convenience of a lunch-room, where well-cooked food can be sold at a reasonable rate, with coziness and attractiveness. The residents believe that substitution is the only remedy against the evils of the saloon. The large kitchen has been carefully equipped, under the direction of Mrs. Ellen Richards, with a New England kitchen outfit, including a number of Aladdin ovens. The foods are carefully prepared, and are sold by the quart or pound to families for home consumption. Coffee, soups, and stews are delivered every day at noon to the neighboring factories. By means of an indurated-fiber can it is possible to transport and serve the food hot. The employees purchase a pint of soup or coffee, with two rolls, for five cents, and the plan of noon factory delivery is daily growing in popularity. The kitchen has been supplying hot lunches at ten cents each to the two hundred women employed in the sewing-room established by the Emergency Committee of the Chicago Women's Club.

A Ward Book and Maps, an Eight-hour Club, the Workingpeople's Social Science Club, the Chicago Question Club, the Nineteenth Ward Improvement Club, a Coöperative Association, a Women's Club, children's clubs, sewing-school, cooking and nature classes, summer excursions, free kindergarten and day-nursery, gymnasium, Men's Club, Temporary Lodging-house, a public dispensary, a labor bureau, and a playground are the various channels through which the life of the House is poured into the neighborhood.*

* "Hull House, a Social Settlement: An Outline Sketch," has been made the basis of the above account. This pamphlet may be obtained by applying to the settlement, 335 South Halsted Street. The brochure is illuminated by photogravures indicating the typical activities of the House.

THE YOUNG PEOPLE'S SOCIETY OF CHRISTIAN ENDEAVOR

President,
FRANCIS E. CLARK, D.D.

General Secretary,
JOHN WILLIS BAER,
646 Washington Street,
Boston, Mass.

Among the marvels of the present age is the great rapidity with which any organization of sterling worth commends itself to one community and then extends to other nations, until it justifies the term "international." The above Society is the very best illustration of this principle. In its early days the furor of extension led to the organization of the numerous societies all over the United States; but the time came when this idea ceased to satisfy. Then, too, the purely spiritual side of its work led to self-complacency and the consciousness that there was somewhat lacking to an all-round development. There were those who feared that very many of the societies would burn themselves out from a lack of fresh fuel. These fears have been rendered groundless, because in 1893 the idea was infused into the order that the time had come for the Christian manhood and womanhood to assert themselves by gaining information about the conditions of their civic life and then applying their knowledge to a bettering of civic conditions. This fact gives a profound significance to the overthrow of municipal misrule, because there is now a large and growing body of young men and women who are determined that the conditions under which municipal misrule alone can flourish shall not be duplicated. The secretary of the Society informs me regarding the inception of this new movement in behalf of civic righteousness:

"While holding to the fundamental principles of Christian Endeavor, President Francis E. Clark, at the Montreal convention in 1893, strongly urged some advance steps for members of Christian Endeavor Societies, one of which was the cultivation of a larger and more intelligent spirit of patriotism and good citizenship. Right nobly did the young people rally around this standard, and at the Cleveland convention a splendid report of progress was made, from which we glean that Christian Endeavor stands for the election of good men, for the enactment of good laws, for steady opposition to the saloon, the gambling-hell, the lottery, the violation of the Sabbath; that it stands by such men as Charles H. Parkhurst, and for kindred spirits in all politics that seek to purify party and make this Immanuel's land.

"More vigorous than ever has been the acceptance of these advance steps by the Societies since the Cleveland convention. It is earnestly hoped that the Christian Endeavor Societies and the members will continue to succeed in keeping their organization from being the tail of any political kite. We are not expecting to join one party, nor is the movement to be partizan in any way. Those of us that are voters are expected to go to the caucus of our party and stand for good men and good measures and always against bad men and bad measures; to stand for good citizenship everywhere, and to exert every ounce of our influence for the right. Many of our members not having yet reached their majority, the work is largely to be educative, and all of it is to be under the guidance of the pastor and church of which every Christian Endeavor Society is a subordinate part."

THE CHRISTIAN CITIZENSHIP LEAGUE

President,
   EDWIN D. WHEELOCK.

Secretary,
   HON. A. M. HASWELL,
      99 Washington Street,
         Chicago, Ill.

This League was organized in April, 1894, the step being taken as a result of the famous Montreal convention of the

Y. P. S. C. E. in 1893. The secretary receives a certain monetary compensation, but also does a great amount of voluntary work. Its constitution is a very short one, with this statement concerning its purpose: "Its object shall be to educate the public conscience, and to secure more generous support for all movements which make for the public welfare." There is only one class of members—active. An executive committee of seven meets at the call of the chairman. Regarding the general scope and policy of the League its president writes:

"We seek to educate and agitate; to exalt Christian ideals; to make Christian principles operative in public affairs; to exalt the name of Christ. Our work is mainly among Christians, and our plea is for loyalty to Christ in public affairs. We aim to build foundations of righteous sentiment which shall give strength to every reform. We are not attempting work which is already being attempted by other organizations. We incite Christians to give hearty support to all such organizations. If they fail in any particular line we shall organize on that line. At each election we shall to some extent organize by wards and precincts for *good men*.

"We are now arranging for systematic study, by the Young People's Societies of Christian Endeavor throughout the State, of topics bearing on citizenship and civic matters. Chicago is, for this purpose, divided into sections or precincts, containing four to eight young people's societies. They will meet monthly in union meetings, with some good speaker to present the topic, and follow with open parliament. In the city and State all young people's societies and churches are invited to coöperate and attend. The *Golden Rule* is about to publish a series of studies on these lines. The hope of all these reforms lies in the organized Christian youth."

The League is not restricted in its political action, and women are eligible to membership. Among the results actually accomplished was a campaign of five hundred meetings in

March, 1894, and in general the awakening of an interest in public affairs by getting Christian men to attend their caucuses and primaries. In the Christian Citizenship campaign its character will be seen from the platform:

"The highest type of citizenship is that which firmly stands for those things in public affairs which are right in the sight of God, and therefore for the highest good of the people, the, city and nation.

"The term 'Christian Citizenship' excludes no one, but, on the contrary, embraces all, of whatever party or creed, who take such a stand.

"This campaign is not political, in the ordinary acceptation of the term, its object being to educate and stimulate the public conscience, and to crystallize Christian sentiment into united and immediate activity against the forces of evil.

"The work is against such candidates, officials, and laws as are corrupt, and therefore contrary to the civil welfare. It is against everything which promotes poverty, corruption, and crime, and in support of everything which would prevent these evils.

"While it pulls off its coat to combat present evils in the most effective ways, it also seeks to lay foundations of righteous public sentiment which shall be for the general good in all time."

UNION FOR PRACTICAL PROGRESS

For a long time the feeling has been prevalent that there was a need for some kind of a "clearing-house" for the various organizations engaged in humanizing work, in order that duplication of effort might be avoided and a greater measure of usefulness brought to bear on those for whom the various societies are laboring.

The Union for Practical Progress is an attempt to unite the

moral forces of society for simultaneous action once each month on some one definite reform measure. In each community where there is a branch Union the clergy are invited to preach on the second Sunday of each month upon the regular monthly topic, and the various labor unions and humanitarian bodies are asked to pass favorable resolutions. Now a hundred reformers are advocating a hundred different reforms at the same time, and to the average mind this whole moral enthusiasm is no more than a medley. The new Union aims to introduce method where chaos now prevails, and of this great mob of moral forces to produce a disciplined army of righteousness.

Mr. B. O. Flower, of Boston, has been the guiding spirit of the Union, and has also been largely responsible for the general policy that has been elaborated in detail by the local Unions. According to the constitution, the purpose of the Union is "to unite all moral forces, agencies, and persons for concerted, methodical, and persistent endeavor in behalf of the public good, and especially for the abolition of unjust social conditions." The actual working out of this purpose is illustrated by the Baltimore Union.

UNION FOR PUBLIC GOOD

Secretary,
MISS A. L. GRAFFLIN,
1123 St. Paul Street,
Baltimore, Md.

The organization of moral forces in Baltimore was first suggested at a meeting of the Ministerial Union, in March, 1893. In the June following the Union for Public Good was organized, and the constitution, adopted by representatives of sixty-three churches, societies, and labor unions, the number having since increased to eighty. It originated in the need felt by all honest people for concentrated action against the organized forces of evil when in control of the machinery of government. It was agreed to bury all sectarian and political differences and to make the moral welfare of the community the sole aim of the association. Men of all creeds and of no creed came together and have since worked enthusiastically to combat some of the recognized evils of society.

Each affiliated society is represented by three delegates, these delegates being the media of communication between the Union and the workers. When the Child-labor Bill was before the Assembly the moral sentiment of the community was not only aroused, but brought to bear actively upon the question through the efforts of these delegates—the Union's responsible representatives in the labor unions and many of the churches. Petitions were circulated and a large deputation sent to Annapolis to urge the measure and mark the enemies of public morality. Without this concentrated action it is very certain that the bill would have been lost.

At the first annual meeting, November, 1893, the president, Mr. C. J. Bonaparte, declared that "our first great achievement must be—to live." "Before proceeding to make Baltimore perfect we must perfect our own organization and secure recognition as a factor in municipal life. That has been accomplished, and the Union can show besides as its fruits the Anti-Sweating and Anti-Child-labor bills. The next and more difficult duty will be to see them enforced. It is the future policy of the Union to aid in purifying municipal politics by organizing the reform element in each ward."

The object of the society, as stated in its constitution, is "to promote the good government, health, and prosperity of Baltimore; to secure useful and prevent injurious legislation; to correct public scandals and abuses; to restrain vice; and to encourage the coöperation of individuals and existing societies to advance these ends." Women are eligible to membership.

IV

WOMEN'S WORK IN MUNICIPAL REFORM

The city means both the place and the population. Each influences the other. In an important sense the place makes the people, and in a more important sense the people make the place. Both the people and the place, then, enter into the problem of the city. That problem, so far as the place is concerned, is to make the city serve in the highest possible degree the physical, intellectual, and moral health of the people. So far as the population is concerned, the problem of the city is to secure the noblest possible manhood and womanhood.

But this may be said to be the great problem of the city and of civilization always and everywhere, while there are certain distinctive problems of the city whose solution is peculiarly difficult in the United States, and, as we shall see, especially urgent at the present time. There are many subordinate problems or factors which enter into the one great problem, but there are two which because of their overshadowing importance will occupy our attention in this discussion, viz., municipal government and city evangelization.

DR. JOSIAH STRONG.

IV

WOMEN'S WORK IN MUNICIPAL REFORM

WITHIN recent years the movements in behalf of the reform of our city governments have been organized and directed by men. Of late the feeling is obtaining in the community that the women are and should be interested in the welfare of their city. Accordingly many of the organizations are inviting their active coöperation, as in the case of the Civic Federation of Chicago; while, on the other hand, the women are forming societies exclusively of their own sex, illustrated by the Woman's Municipal League of New York. That the women exerted an influence in the overthrow of ring rule and the establishment of good government is conceded by the share that they had in the election of Mayor Schieren, of Brooklyn, in 1893. At the municipal election in New York in 1894 the vigorous campaign conducted by the Woman's Municipal League, by means of public meetings held in those sections of the municipality that are usually abandoned to the ward politician and his heelers, aroused an interest in civic affairs on the part of the women; and the reflex influence of this influence manifested itself at the polls by the ballots that the men cast for instead of against good government. Other organizations of women did not take such an active part in politics, but have aimed to instruct their members in the knowledge of civics. This they accomplish by regular class-work and parlor meetings. The influence of the women who are members of the various young people's societies in the churches is beginning to exert a very appreciable effect in what makes for good citizenship, because they are informing themselves regarding their rights and duties as members of the body politic.

THE CIVIC CLUB OF PHILADELPHIA.

President,   *Secretary*,
MRS. CORNELIUS STEPHENSON.   MISS CORNELIA FROTHINGHAM,
2035 Walnut Street,
Philadelphia, Pa.

This Club was organized in January, 1894, with a voluntary secretary. An annual fee of $3 is required from each member, and since January 1, 1894, an initiation fee of $5 has been required. Fifteen members comprise the executive committee, which meets on the last Monday in the month. Four departments summarize the work, namely:

1. Municipal Government.   3. Social Science.
2. Education.   4. Art.

This work is further apportioned among sub-committees. The Club has no organ of its own, but works through groups of people, wherever they are banded together in some kind of organization. The secretary writes:

"We women believe that serious permanent results can only be obtained through *education*. And acting upon this belief, we intend to devote ourselves to the collecting of such facts as bear upon the development of disinterested citizenship; to the teaching of such thoughts as are likely to raise the moral and intellectual standards of our community; and to the urging upon all educators, whether public or private, the uncompromising introduction of such teaching in every school."

The object of the society, as stated in its constitution, "shall be to promote by education and active coöperation a higher public spirit and a better social order." A membership of four hundred in August, 1894, attested the response to this call to action. Of necessity the field for direct political action is restricted. The Civic Club is not a political body; neither does it propose to undertake special work already well done by other organizations, but, on the contrary, to lend its support to and coöperate with those useful organizations now engaged upon work in various fields; bringing together disconnected interests and causing each individual effort to become the manifestation of a higher and more disinterested patriotism.

THE CIVITAS CLUB

President,
MISS JESSIE S. DIKE.

Secretary,
MISS EDNA S. DOUGHTY,
289 Washington Avenue,
Brooklyn, N. Y.

This Club was organized in November, 1893, just before the election of the reform ticket, and had for its object the awakening of public spirit and interest within the circles of its influence. A voluntary secretary directs the work. "Our membership consists of two hundred young women from the leading families of our city, and many of them have become keenly alive to questions of public interest and have already exerted a noble influence among their friends who, while holding the privilege of the ballot, feel no responsibility in regard to its use. We have also a well-initiated philanthropic work among the incapable children of the Kings County Hospital, and are advancing now in several other directions which demand attention and improvement." The object of the Club is to awaken an interest in matters pertaining to municipal welfare, and to seek a better social order. The annual dues are $3. An executive committee of fifteen meets once a week and apportions the work among the various standing committees:

1. General Municipal Improvement.
2. Government and Courts.
3. General Philanthropy.
4. Class-work and Sociological Study.

Women only are eligible to membership, of which the limit is two hundred. The Club is not restricted in its political action. One of the members writes me:

"One member secured seven votes for the last election. Not all voted along the line of *her* conviction, but it was something to induce several men who had never cared to cast a ballot before to perform the duty of a citizen."

This list of topics for study will indicate the practical nature of the educational work:

1. Education in our City.
    (1) Public Schools.
    (2) Private Schools.
    (3) The Pratt Institute.
2. Musical Advantages of our City.
3. Art Advantages of our City.
4. The Newspapers of Brooklyn.
5. The Amusements of Brooklyn.
6. The Clubs of Brooklyn.
7. The Government and Courts of Brooklyn.
8. The Social Life of Brooklyn.
9. The Churches and Missions of Brooklyn.
10. The Philanthropic Societies and Hospitals of Brooklyn.
11. The Prisons and Reformatories of Brooklyn.
12. The Health and Cleanliness of Brooklyn.
13. Special features of Brooklyn which differentiate it from other cities and favor its future development.

LADIES' HEALTH PROTECTIVE ASSOCIATION

President,
Mrs. H. S. Bell.

Corresponding Secretary,
Mrs. M. E. Trautmann,
27 Beekman Place,
New York.

Organized November 22, 1884, the Association was incorporated December 9th of the same year. The position of the secretary is voluntary. According to the certificate of incorporation: "The particular business and object of such society is to protect the health of the people of the city of New York by taking such action, from time to time, as may secure the enforcement of existing sanitary laws and regulations by calling the attention of the proper authorities to any violations thereof, and to procure the amendment of said laws and regulations when they shall be found inefficient for the prevention of acts injurious to the public health."

The annual dues are $1. The executive committee numbers fifteen and meets regularly once a month. There are twelve committees, all charged with some phase of sanitary work.

THE MUNICIPAL ORDER LEAGUE OF CHICAGO

President,
Mrs. H. W. Duncanson.

Secretary,
Mrs. S. C. Tobin,
70 Madison Street,
Chicago, Ill.

Organized in 1892, the League was incorporated March, 1894. The secretary receives a nominal salary. An executive committee of seven meets each month, and if necessary oftener, at the call of the president. There are three classes of members—honorary, associate, and working; honorary members pay an annual fee of $5, and active, $1. The departments of work are:

1. Membership.
2. Bath-house.
3. Drinking-fountains.
4. Rubbish-boxes.
5. Program.
6. Park-lighting.
7. Street-car Spitting.
8. Street Beggars and Cripples.

The society has no organ of its own, but comes in touch with its workers by means of reports presented at the monthly meetings. There is no political restriction in the work of the League.

"The women of Chicago were suffering in their homes from poor city service. After making individual attempts to better the conditions, and failing, but believing that 'in union there is strength,' they called a mass-meeting in Central Music-hall and invited all citizens to attend. The meeting was well attended, and there was at once formed what has since been known as the Municipal Order League. The members are not all women, though the officers happen to be. It is simply an organization of citizens whose chief aim is to better the sanitary condition of Chicago. The business men of this city seem to be too much engrossed in their private affairs to give this subject much attention, so the burden of the work has been given to the women. By appealing to our Chicago women's love for home, by interesting them in the surroundings, we have brought to our ranks the right kind of women and made possible much that could not have been accomplished without such interest."

The object of the association is to promote the healthfulness, cleanliness, and beauty of Chicago, and the securing of certain public improvements. It shall keep clear of all political or party complications. Its work shall be from year to year, according to the peculiar needs of the times, its main business being to promote intelligent coöperation between the people and the people's officers in cleaning and keeping clean the streets of Chicago. Accomplished results have been the appropriation by the city of a sum of money sufficient to equip a free public bath, and the permission of the League to nominate the attendant. This was the only free public bath in the city in 1894. Drinking-fountains have been opened in various parts of the city. Individual reports on unsanitary places have led to the abatement of the nuisance. The individuals of the League have been educated in a knowledge of municipal affairs, so that they are cognizant of their duties as well as their rights.

The League had an inspector, whose duty it was to visit the alleys in a prescribed district and report to it, while the society took the matter before the proper city authorities. The result has been most encouraging, because the heads of departments had no longer the excuse of not being able to ascertain the exact conditions.

PHILADELPHIA BRANCH OF THE NATIONAL WOMEN'S HEALTH PROTECTIVE ASSOCIATION

President,
MRS. JOHN H. SCRIBNER.

Secretary,
MISS COCKROFT,
4433 Sansom Street,
Philadelphia, Pa.

"A small class in social science, composed of members of the New Century Club, felt that the city needed such a society, and invited Mrs. Trautmann, of the New York Health Protective Association, to give us an idea of the work of their Association. The society started with about twenty members and now has about two hundred. We use no money, except for postals and for the only salary paid—$20 per month to the secretary of the Complaint Bureau—and this is contributed by special arrangement with friends interested in the work. The Complaint Bureau was organized to receive complaints of nuisances existing in any portion of the city, to be investigated as far as possible, and then reported to the proper department. This bureau has done valuable work in keeping garbage-collectors up to their duties and in causing policemen to be more alert in reporting unsanitary conditions. We have the cordial coöperation of the heads of the departments, which makes our public work easier. We propose having a representative in every election district, who shall investigate every complaint of an objectionable or unsanitary condition existing in her district. Our most *important* effort is to create in our members a sense of *individual* responsibility."

The society was organized, with a voluntary secretary, in the spring of 1893. It is not incorporated. The membership fees are $1 a year. There is no separate executive committee, but the whole body meets each week, while the public is invited to the monthly meetings. The departments of work thus far are:

1. Street-cleaning.
2. The Sweating System.
3. Garbage.
4. Water-supply.

The society has no organ of its own, but receives a report of progress at each monthly meeting; it is not restricted in its political action.

WOMEN'S HEALTH PROTECTIVE ASSOCIATION OF BROOKLYN

President,
MRS. JAMES SCRINGEOUR.

Secretary,
MRS. EDWIN ATWELL,
1088 Dean Street,
Brooklyn, N. Y.

The Association was organized in March, 1890, and incorporated April 2, 1890, with a voluntary secretary. Annual dues of $1 from each of the four hundred and fifty members support the society. Twenty-five constitute the board of directors, with an executive committee of seven, meeting once a month. The departments of work are:

1. Municipal.
2. Legal.
3. Lecture.
4. Press.
5. House.

The Association has no organ of its own, but comes in touch with its workers, who may attend the monthly meetings of the board of directors. The society is non-partizan and has neighborhood or branch Associations in the election districts. As stated in its constitution, "the objects of this Association shall be to inspire the women of Brooklyn with a realization of their municipal obligations; to promote the health of the people of Brooklyn and the cleanliness of the city by taking such action, from time to time, as may secure the enforcement of existing sanitary laws and regulations by calling the attention of the proper authorities to any violation thereof, and to procure the amendment of such laws and regulations when they shall be found insufficient for the prevention of acts injurious to the public health or the cleanliness of the city."

A few results actually accomplished are cleaner streets, because of boxes for waste placed on the street-corners; cleaner cars, due to placards prohibiting spitting on the floor; increased interest in the cleanliness and health of the city on the part of the women; and the initial movement resulting in the overthrow of the ring rule in 1893.

The Association originated in the thought of its president, who desired to see Brooklyn made a cleaner and more attractive city, through a more patriotic interest on the part of the women. A meeting was called to consider to what extent women are responsible for the condition of the streets, and that conference led to the organization of the Women's Health

Protective Association of Brooklyn, somewhat on the lines of the older Association of the same name in New York.

It has grown steadily in four years, and now numbers four hundred and fifty paying members, while a much larger number are actively engaged in extending its influence and carrying out its principles.

CIVIC LEAGUE

(ORIGINALLY WOMAN'S MUNICIPAL LEAGUE)

President,
   MRS. ROBERT ABBE.

Secretary,
   MRS. CHARLES H. RUSSELL,
                   New York.

In numerous campaign speeches Dr. Parkhurst referred to the great influence which the women of the town could wield in behalf of good government. Finally a few reporters went to Mrs. Josephine Shaw Lowell, to ask if she purposed to lead in what might become an organized movement on the part of the women. She at once replied that she had no time for any new work and had no intention of undertaking any. On reflection, however, she decided that she would be sadly lacking in public spirit if she refused to work for one month in uprooting the chief municipal evils because she was so much occupied in lopping off some of the branches. The next step was the request of an interview with Dr. Parkhurst, and he appointed October 4th, when Mrs. Lowell and her daughter called at his house. In response to her question if he had any definite plan by means of which the women could help, he replied, "No." Mrs. Lowell then asked if he would speak at women's meetings once a week until the election, beginning Friday, October 12th, with an audience invited by card and selected from the "Social Register," because it was Mrs. Lowell's opinion that the up-town women had the least appreciation of their civic duties, and if their interest could be aroused they in turn would arouse the men. Dr. Parkhurst agreed, but suggested in addition that meetings should be held for the down-town women.

The first meeting was accordingly held October 12th, at the Young Men's Christian Association Hall, and three thousand postals were sent in the names of Mrs. Lowell and about thirty managers. Mrs. Lowell invited the managers who were in town to assemble an hour before the meeting for a conference with Dr. and Mrs. Parkhurst, with the result that three committees were chosen: one on down-town meetings, a second on publication, and a third on parlor meetings. It was Mrs. Lowell's intention that the organization should tell women the truth regarding the condition of the city, impress them with the fact that they had duties to the public, and induce the women to make the men of their families realize their political obligations and urge them to do their duty at the coming election. For about a week after the first meeting Mrs. Lowell continued as the leader of the League, until her illness prevented active participation.

In pursuance of the object of the League—to create a sound public opinion—twenty public meetings and fifteen parlor meetings were held. The conferences that were held on the East Side were most helpful, because that part of the community had been neglected by all except the *practical* politicians, and it was noted with what eagerness the response came to the genuine sympathy of the League. Thanks to these efforts it is fair to credit the League with an increase in the registration.

At a meeting, October 19, 1894, these resolutions were adopted:

"WHEREAS, We women, natives, inhabitants, and taxpayers of New York, have a deep interest in the well-being and good name of our city; and

"Whereas, Vice and crime are fostered within her borders, and her name has become a byword among all nations because of the corruption of our city government;

"*Resolved*, That we call upon all men and women who love the right, and who desire for their children pure and noble lives, to work together against the strong power which now controls our city and has bound her hand and foot."

A very practical work was accomplished by means of a wide distribution of leaflets, on a variety of municipal subjects. These were briefly stated, and dealt with the subject in such a way as to carry conviction. One of the most forcible must serve as a type of the others:

WOMAN'S MUNICIPAL LEAGUE

HAVE I ALL MY RIGHTS?

1.

"Is the street in which I live dirty and unhealthy for my children to play in? Yes.

"Then it is because the Tammany city government wastes the money given to make it clean.

2.

"Do I have water enough, especially for flushing the closets?

"If not, it is because the Tammany city government allows it to be wasted, and me to be robbed of that which it is my right to have, by those who *pay* Tammany for it.

3.

"Is there water standing in the cellar which makes my family sick and my doctor's bill big?

"The Health Board of New York is run by Tammany Hall.

4.

"Are the public schools so overcrowded that my children cannot go to school because there is no place for them? They are.

"This is because the Tammany city government wastes the money which I have helped to give to build more schools and hire more teachers.

5.

"Have I been compelled, under threat of arrest or stopping my business, to pay the police for protection in addition to the cost of my license?

"If I have not, many of my friends who keep street-stands, hucksters' wagons, or who are venders of wares of all kinds, have had to do so.

"The police force of New York is run by Tammany Hall.

6.

"Have you read in the newspapers the terrible story of Mrs. Urchittel, and how the police put her in jail and took her business and children away from her?

"If you have not, *do so*, and work hard to turn out the Tammany city government, which allows such things to be done.

7.

"The way to do this is to vote for the ticket headed by William L. Strong and nominated by the Citizens' Committee of Seventy, and to influence your neighbors to do the same."

Another most effective campaign document was the statement of the Russian widow, Cecilia Urchittel.

The object of the League is the promotion of an intelligent public spirit and a better city government. There are four departments of work:

1. Municipal Affairs. This is devoted to examination into the aims and functions of the city government; to the gathering of intelligent reports concerning it; to the suggestion of schemes of improvement; and to the finding of means of coöperation with good citizens outside the League for the carrying out of these schemes.

2. Education. This department will inform itself and the League concerning the condition of public schools in the city, and suggest means of improvement; it shall study the workings of night-schools, free lectures, kindergartens, etc., reporting upon them to the executive board, with a view to raising the standard of instruction and increasing the attendance of pupils and number of schools.

3. Social Science. This will examine into the problems of public health, philanthropy, and social reform, as they affect the citizens of New York, and shall report upon the same to the executive board, and attempt to secure coöperation with all good citizens for the promotion of a higher standard of public health and comfort.

4. Municipal Action. It will fall within the scope of this department to study the conditions which help or hinder the establishment of a high standard of beauty in our parks, pleasure-grounds, statues, fountains, public buildings, and streets, and to carry out whatever schemes of improvement may be approved by the executive board.

THE SOCIETY FOR POLITICAL STUDY

Secretary,
MRS. JEANNETTE N. LEEPER,
256 West Eighty-fourth Street,
New York.

According to its constitution, "its object shall be the study of political science and kindred subjects." It will thus be noted that its object does not concern itself with municipal reform in the narrower sense, but it should certainly be regarded as one factor in the bettering of the city. Its work is educational; but in such efforts there are great potentialities, because many a distinctively reform movement has had its inception in a small company of kindred spirits who have met for the study of social questions. The very fact of their study opens the eyes to the situation and to the need of reform; then it is wisely and intelligently carried out. The theme for 1895 is "Municipal Government," subdivided into these topics: "The Charter;" "The City Electors;" "The City Primaries;" "Elections and Election Laws;" "The Executive Department;" "The Legislative Department;" "Judicial;" "Finance;" "Sanitary Laws;" "Tenement and Lodging Houses;" "Public Parks;" "Amusements;" "Municipal Taxation;" "Penal and Charitable Institutions;" "The Public Schools;" "The Colleges and Universities;" "The Police Department;" "The Saloons and Excise Laws;" "Wall Street;" "Banking and the Clearing-house;" "Transportation;" "Relation of the Churches to the City." At each meeting the paper of the day and the news of the week are discussed and an opportunity given for the study of parliamentary usage.

The origin of the Society was in the need felt by its early members of accurate knowledge concerning politics and the science of government. Its growth has been steady and great. Its object is the attainment of knowledge on certain lines and parliamentary practice.

V

THE CITY VIGILANCE LEAGUE

The city should in every possible way increase the health, safety, convenience, comfort, and happiness of its citizens. Against the business-concern idea of city government we set the idea of the home, the family. The city must be managed as a well-ordered household, and should do for its citizens everything that a private individual or corporation cannot do better. Though there are cynics who say that lack of principle is the chief characteristic of business, we have no quarrel with business principles as such. We need them, of course, in the well-governed city, just as in the well-ordered household.

The need of the moment, then, is a practical and inspiring positive program. On the other hand, we said a positive program means good government. Negative criticism is good, but it can only lead to a mere garnishing of the chamber; the one spirit of corruption driven out will return with seven other spirits worse than the first. To prevent this, sustained enthusiasm is necessary, and this nothing but a positive program will give. Experience in Europe and America shows that only the enlarged idea of the functions of a city can keep up in the citizens that continual interest necessary to check corruption. Limit in every way the powers of city officials to do evil, and you limit their powers to do good; intrust to the city no great interest, and the citizens will have no great interest in the city. Give the city great power, great responsibility, and great undertakings, and the citizens, for very fear of the terrible results of corruption, will keep the administration clean.

WILLIAM SCUDAMORE.

V

THE CITY VIGILANCE LEAGUE

President,
C. H. PARKHURST.

Secretary,
WILLIAM HOWE TOLMAN,
427 West Fifty-seventh Street,
New York.

It has been the aim of this publication to present the general objects and methods of the various reform movements in all parts of the country, so that a community desirous of effecting any kind of an organization may select and combine those features that will best subserve local needs. After selection and combination, how may an organization be best effected in order to concentrate the forces making for good government? We may assume that some one personality will be prominent; that some one man will be interested in the civic welfare to such an extent that he will be willing to devote time and labor to secure it. Such a person will naturally lead, and will take the initiative. In the first place, he should make a thorough study of local conditions, in order that he may be able to answer questions which will surely be put to him; and, secondly, he should make a comparative study of how other cities are working for municipal reform. The leader can get all the necessary data by sending to the secretaries for an exhibit of the work of their organizations. Following out these two lines of investigation, the leader will have the necessary self-information for the next step, which will be a carefully chosen conference of representatives from the leading existing forces which are, or which should be, making for good government. This conference should be very select—that is, only men should be brought together who will agree along a few definite lines. The leader can select his men by personal interviews, and then a personal invitation should be extended, in order that they may be sure to attend. Thus a unity will be given to the initial conference, and when it is adjourned the same general plan of campaign will be discussed in the community. The leader should so have made himself master of local conditions and methods of work that he can guide the deliberations toward an end which the experience of other cities has shown to be wise. Let him have several suggestions which he can use tentatively; but he must be clear in his own mind on the general principles which should guide such work.

The place where the initial conference is held is very important, because a reform movement, to have the greatest measure of success, must include all the divergent elements of the civic life; and to the extent to which any one is omitted, to that extent is its usefulness impaired. With the thought that the movement must be non-sectarian and non-partizan, a place must be selected which will give no local color to the meeting. The coöperation of organized labor is all-important, and some of their halls might form a neutral ground. With the above thoughts in mind, certain difficulties will be obviated from the outset.

The initial conference will be most fruitful in affording an object-lesson to those who may attend, whereby the ignorance of their civic knowledge will be painfully apparent. To prove that, let the leader ask them in what ward they live, who is their Assemblyman, what was the city budget for the last fiscal year, and so on. In fact, it would be a good idea for the leader to propound a few questions from a "shorter catechism in civics" which he might prepare. The very fact of lamentable ignorance will be a spur to each one to seek civic information, and a demand will arise for a second conference. Then the circle can very well be enlarged.

At the second conference those who came to the first will have sufficiently informed themselves as to local conditions, so that they can discuss ways and means based on organizations in other cities. Let there be a free and thorough comparative study of the methods. I would suggest that at the second conference one committee be chosen to nominate permanent officers, and another to prepare a statement of the object of the formation of the municipal reform organization, and also to submit the draft of a plan of work. When the third meeting is held a plan of work will be sufficiently definite for a membership committee to be appointed. Up to this point it is urged that the conferences be small, because a few energetic men who think alike can be much more successful in shaping and inaugurating the movement than a large number of persons with no definite ideas. For a name, the "Municipal Reform League of ——," or the "City Vigilance League," is suggested.

By the time that the name has been selected, permanent officers chosen, and plans for definite lines of work mapped out, there is then no reason why a constructive campaign should not be opened. At the outset this policy should ever be borne in mind: that the movement must be positive and constructive rather than negative and destructive. This does not mean that there shall be no tearing down, but that stress shall be laid on the upbuilding.

After the organization is effected, members must be gathered in. One effective way is by sending out pledge-cards containing a brief statement of what any good citizen would at once admit should characterize good government. As fast as signatures to the pledge-cards come in they should be acknowledged, and the enthusiasm of the signers be crystallized into action by assigning to each one some definite, concrete work, even if it be nothing more than counting the schools and churches in his particular area. Some method must be devised for the secretary or the executive committee to come in touch with the workers, because that bond must be vital and persistent. One method of communication is by means of monthly bulletins. The first bulletins will contain the aim and scope of the organization, with the district leader to whom each member is responsible. It is always well to follow the existing municipal divisions, rather than carve out new administrative areas for work. An excellent method of securing an executive council or committee is to form it of the leaders of the wards or the Assembly districts, according to whichever area forms a grand division. These bulletins should also contain a brief set of questions, for the double purpose of arousing the interest of the members and of affording data for the use of the executive committee.

Two bulletins should be sent to each member, and after the information has been secured, one should be returned to the executive committee and the other to the local leader. By that means both the local leader and the organization are informed of the civic conditions. In succeeding bulletins brief extracts of the law may be quoted—for instance, a very few lines can give the substance of the excise law, and so on. Then, too, the bulletin affords opportunity to give a collective answer to questions which may be sent in by the various members. There should be a series of questions in each number, so that there may be something to do, and at the same time the answerer will be gaining an increasing fund of information regarding his city. The questions should also be more difficult —that is, they should require keener attention and observation.

The officer who will be largely responsible for the life of the organization will be the secretary, because he will be the one to come in touch with the community at many and varying points. The card-catalogue system is the best for recording the membership. Each card should contain a line for the name, address—both office and home—church, denomination, society, Assembly and election district. Cards containing this data are easy to handle, and make a very convenient mailing-list. In continuance of the aim of this book the work of the League will be described in detail, and concrete illustrations of its administrative methods will be given, so that they may serve as an object-lesson in effecting similar organizations, because experience has proved their adaptability; hence their adoption and extension in other localities are perfectly feasible.

In April, 1892, delegates from a young men's organization in the various churches of New York and Brooklyn met in the regular monthly meeting at the Madison Square Church to discuss problems of good citizenship. Dr. Parkhurst was invited to address them on that subject, but could give them only a very brief talk, as he had another engagement that same evening. Such a profound impression was made by his lofty tone and his earnest words that the young men unanimously resolved that they would invite him to deliver a second address and make possible a larger audience. Accordingly the Scottish Rite Hall was engaged in May, 1892. This meeting had been planned for by a committee which was appointed by the young men of the Madison Square Church. The subject of the doctor's address was along the same lines, namely, an appeal to the civic manhood of the young men. The meeting was presided over by Mr. L. L. Delafield.

So much enthusiasm had been aroused by these two meetings and the succeeding events that an organization was effected, but on a very small scale, as about a dozen of the young men met in weekly gatherings. The all-absorbing question of a name for the society was occupying the minds of all; but when no decision could be agreed upon one of their number decided that he would cable Dr. Parkhurst—who had gone abroad for his summer vacation—and ask him to suggest a name. The cable reached the doctor at Vevay and was the subject of a great deal of thought, for he realized that the matter of the name which should express the intent of what such an organization should represent was very important. After careful reflection, as he was thinking of the great need of watchfulness if the society was to accomplish the greatest measure of usefulness, the word "vigilance" occurred to him. "Just the thing," he said to himself; "it must be an organization banded together for vigilance in civic affairs." Then the rest of the combination was comparatively easy, and the telegraph flashed the words to New York: *The City Vigilance League.* Among the members in the formative period of the League were W. P. Young, C. E. Lawton, C. A. B. Pratt, A. S. Lyman, R. McA. Lloyd, W. M. Kingsley, and R. H. Robinson.

The autumn of 1892 and the early part of the following year were devoted to the extension of the League by means of meetings held in various parts of the city and usually addressed by the doctor, in order to explain the origin and scope of the League. The methods of extension were about the same as at the present, but the League grew in numbers very slowly. As it has proved, this was the best thing that could have happened, for those who did ally themselves with the movement did so because they believed in it and were willing to devote themselves to it for the sake of the city. Accordingly the small membership was instrumental in developing a strong and intelligent purpose that would persevere in the face of obstacles and aspersions. It so chanced that Dr. Parkhurst was also the president of the Society for the Prevention of Crime, and was then coming into very prominent notice on account of the means which he thought were the best in the furtherance of his particular object—namely, the securing of legal proofs of the existence of crime and the collusion of the police with the violation of the law. Moral proof he already had, but he needed that kind of proof that would be received in a court of law.

In the early history of the League, its methods and general policy were very nebulous. The immediate need was to secure the coöperation of an earnest body of young men who were willing to *do* something for their city; just what channel was to serve as the means of utilizing this activity was uncertain. The policy of the League has shaped itself as definite, concrete needs have arisen. When that which was tentative in dealing with a particular problem showed itself to be successful, it was woven into its general line of action and extended so as to grapple with all the phases of the problem in question. In an historical sketch of the League, with the above facts in mind, when there were very few leaders working in coöperation or under the direction of Dr. Parkhurst, this letter, written by him in July, 1892, to one of the officers of the League, will indicate that no clear line of action had been formulated by him. It is of interest that the present policy of the organization is a development of the germs of action in that letter:

"The object of our movement is expressed in the name of our organization—the City Vigilance League. There is nothing of which the city of New York stands more in need in order to its improvement and civic reconstruction, than a thorough understanding and consciousness of its present character. It does not avail a great deal to indulge in rhetorical pyrotechnics regarding the political corruption of the town. Oratory is cheap, and any amount of it can be had for a low figure. There is nothing so significant as facts. If I have at all succeeded in stirring up the town it is because I have given facts. Now that is the key-note of any policy that is to prove availing to the improvement of our city and to the maintenance of its improved condition when once that improvement has been secured. In other words, the town must know itself, and

I want simply one thoroughly-in-earnest man for each election district that will help me to do it. That is what I have meant all the way along when I have said that with a thousand such men I could accomplish the civic renovation of New York. It is perfectly feasible—I know it can be done. The experience of the last six months demonstrates it. Watchfulness is the price of liberty.

"I think this will make clear the difference between what we are undertaking and what was undertaken by the Municipal League. Our enterprise contemplates nothing less than that the representative of each election district should be able to state authoritatively everything that is going on in that district. Now of course that means a great deal. It does not necessarily mean that he should have to behold with his own eyes everything that is transpiring there, but that, by some means or other, he should gain the information that should enable him to speak with unquestionable authority. As I said before, this is feasible. It can be done and must be done, and the City Vigilance League is the organization to do it. I cannot conceive of a greater work that a thousand of our best, brightest, and most earnest young men can do for New York than just that which I have outlined. It cannot be done in a day or a month, but the eyes of our whole country are upon us, and what we do in New York we shall, in a way, be doing for every city similarly constituted.

"There is nothing political about this, and nothing that has immediate reference to the polls; but it will all contribute to political results, and from year to year will become determinative of political November issues. I am very anxious, therefore, that the committee should push forward as rapidly as it can the work of fixing upon picked men and acquainting them with the real purpose of the movement as above outlined. You will see how perfectly coincident the purpose of this League is with that of the Society for the Prevention of Crime, as illustrated by the work which the Society has been doing during the last four months.

"I want to guard the committee against the idea that our thousand young men are to engage in exactly the sort of work which I have found it necessary, in a few instances, to put my own hand to. Our enemies are so disposed to make capital out of those matters that our policy and actions must be wise and guarded. There will be enough, however, that we can do, and ways enough of doing it, without laying ourselves open to the necessity of accusation, and without working moral detriment to those who may be participants in the enterprise. It wants to be a constant thought with us that what we have undertaken is an immense work, and that success will be determined in the issue far more by the quality and thoroughness of what we do than by its quantity."

In the autumn of 1892 it was necessary to take up the work, which had been sadly interrupted on account of the dispersion incident to the summer. By that time the methods were slowly crystallizing, and were stated in this circular, which will be read with interest by those who have recently joined the League:

"The time has now arrived when it is practicable to lay down in fuller detail the lines along which the work of this society will require to be prosecuted. Immediately subsequent to its organization in May, 1892, the annual summer dispersion rendered temporary suspension necessary, and little was accomplished before the 1st of October, except to mature plans of organization and of effort. Those upon whose sympathy and coöperation we can count are now for the most part returned to town, and the way is open for realizing our purposes with promptness and effect.

"It was stated in a letter written to the City Vigilance League from Switzerland, under date of July 3d, that 'there is nothing of which the city of New York stands more in need, for its improvement and civic reconstruction, than a thorough understanding and consciousness of its own character.' General as is the impression that things here are not as they ought to be, and that the administration of our city is vested in the criminal classes and in their sympathizers and abettors, there is nevertheless not that detailed knowledge of the concrete facts in the case that is necessary in order that the matter may come home with power and effect to the intelligence and the conscience of the community at large. Now it is that condition of things exactly that creates the necessity for such an organization as the Vigilance League. We have no political aim whatever; our only ambition is thoroughly to know our city and to make the facts that concern its character and maladministration distinctly discernible and easily appreciable to the average mind, regardless of the political or the religious differences that may happen to subsist among us.

"The governmental reconstruction of this city is sooner or later to be accomplished, and when that result comes it will come as the effect of bringing out into the light facts that are already known to some, suspected by many, and adroitly and painstakingly kept under cover by the salaried criminals whom we are paying to attend to our municipal interests. Facts are the agency by which results are to be wrought, and it is the *facts*, therefore, to which we need first of all to address ourselves.

"From what has been already said it will be seen that the policy proposed is one of persistency and thoroughness. Anything that is worth working for at all is worth working for a good while and with a careful regard to details. Our immediate need is of 1137 men of honest spirit and durable stuff (whether Democrats or Republicans makes not a whit of difference, if they are zealous for a clean city government) who will undertake to represent respectively each of the election districts into which this city is subdivided. It will be the responsibility of each one of these 1137 men to make himself thoroughly conversant with all that concerns the district under his charge. He must *know* his district through and through.

"The first duty of the district supervisor will be to prepare a careful and accurate chart of his district. In order that uniformity may be secured it is desired that these charts shall be drawn on the scale of twenty-five feet to the inch. Every building must be represented on the chart, with its proportional frontage and its proper street number. With the map thus drawn there is furnished a basis upon which to put all matters of fact pertaining to the district, so fast as such facts shall be accumulated.

"The first thing to learn and tabulate will be the occupants of the residential portions of the districts—their names and nationality, with the number and names of voters in each, and whether the voters respectively are native American or naturalized. In those cases where the occupant is not the owner of the premises the name and address of the owner should be secured.

"Buildings used for other than residential purposes must be dealt with in the same detailed way and their character indicated on the chart. This will include churches, with an accumulation of all the facts pertaining to them that would be serviceable in making a complete statement as to their character and condition, such as denomination, numerical strength, etc. The same attention will require to be paid to schools, to saloons, a full account of which latter will include such items as the name of the brewer under whose patronage the saloon is run; the general character of the place; the relations subsisting between it and the policeman on the beat or the captain of the precinct; whether it is kept open in illegal hours, or whether it sells to minors; whether it has a license, and if so when its license expires, etc., together with any other facts that may be essential to a complete account of the matter. It hardly needs to be said that the survey and tabulation must include a statement as to all houses of prostitution, pool-rooms and policy-shops, and gambling-houses in the district. In this connection, however, it is expressly urged that no district supervisor should do anything that can be construed as compromising his own moral character. In all that relates to houses of prostitution in particular too great caution in this respect cannot be used. The Society for the Prevention of Crime and its detectives can be availed of in assisting supervisors to a knowledge of the facts in cases of that description.

"The attention of supervisors will also have to be directed to whatever concerns the condition of the streets in their districts respectively, such as their cleanliness, how often swept, the collection of garbage, and whether such collection is made regularly and promptly; also the condition of the paving, and, in cases where paving is being laid, whether it is being laid according to contract.

"These references will suffice to indicate the character of the work that is to be undertaken. It is perfectly feasible, although it will require fidelity, persistency, and ingenuity. As the supervisors go on in their work they will acquire facility and will discover means of reaching results that will not, perhaps, occur to them till after they have put their hands to the undertaking. Communications will be made to the supervisors from time to time, either by the president directly or through representatives that will be selected to care for the interests of the *Assembly* districts respectively, and suggestions made as to methods of working and as to certain kinds of assistance that can be afforded in the matter of gathering the necessary details.

"The above specifications by no means cover the entire work that will be prosecuted by the City Vigilance League, but will suffice for present purposes, and will serve amply to illustrate our spirit and intent, which is that *wherever the administrative blood beats in this city the finger of the Vigilance League shall be upon it counting its pulsations.*

"C. H. PARKHURST, *President.*"

In order that the summer of 1893 might not necessitate the beginning over again in the autumn, and that the work might be extended by the members of the League who were in town, the services of an organizing secretary were secured. Meetings and conferences were held by him so as to effect the organization of the Assembly districts. A circular letter issued that summer gave a brief *résumé* of the work up to that time:

NEW YORK CITY, August, 1893.

"We have now just completed the first year of our history. Between four and five hundred men are already actually at work in the field. Operations have been commenced in twenty-two out of the thirty Assembly districts. *Whatever concerns the interests of our city is made subject of inquiry and conference.* The tendency among all our larger cities is to allow matters of municipal administration to drift into the hands of men who conceive of positions of official trust as means of access to the public treasury. The fault is chargeable as well to those who permit this prostitution of power as to those who practise it. The League aims to counteract this tendency, and to stimulate, among young men especially, an intelligent and earnest civic consciousness, by giving to each member some line of investigation to prosecute, some field of duty to cover. In this way a great variety of questions have arisen for consideration, each of which tends to bring the 'Leaguer' into immediate relations with his city, and in that way to set him studying existing conditions as a means of improving those conditions. In one Assembly district, for example, the Sunday violation of excise laws is being observed and investigated; in another the 'sweating' problem; and in a third the truck and sidewalk encumbrance nuisance. All of these questions are being considered in their bearings upon the interests of the city at large. The impression which widely prevailed for a time that the League is an organization of amateur detectives has become pretty thoroughly dissipated. *We are trying to bring into coöperant relations a great company of earnest young citizens who believe in inoculating foreign-born residents with American impulses; in encouraging every influence that will make for our municipal betterment; and in giving currency to the doctrine that for city officials to impose taxes and to drain off a considerable percentage of the proceeds of such assessment into their own pockets falls a good way short of the ideal of municipal government."*

Very early in the history of the League, particularly when it was trying to win the confidence of the community and ward off the attacks of its enemies, some method of communication between the executive committee and the members was needed. In order to come in touch with the Leaguers monthly bulletins were issued. These served a double purpose: information was obtained, and the Leaguer who obtained it was at the same time gaining a knowledge of his own city, whereby his civic consciousness was made more keen. The chief purpose of these bulletins was their educational character. It will be noted that they were progressive; each one is more difficult, that is, it requires keener observation and more patience in eliciting the necessary information. The bulletins were issued in duplicate, the Assembly leader retaining one for his own use, so as to be in possession of the facts regarding his district, and sending the other to the general secretary of the League. The League now has a monthly journal of its own—the *City Vigilant*. Some kind of a bulletin issued at stated intervals is imperative for holding and stimulating the interest of the members.

THE CITY VIGILANCE LEAGUE

BULLETIN NO. I.

JANUARY, 1893.

To........................,

Supervisor of Election District No....

DEAR SIR: It has been thought wise that once in three weeks a bulletin should be issued to all the members of the League, in order that we may come into touch with one another, and the lines along which we are working be made easier and more distinct. Recruits are being brought into the field, and the work is progressing; but a part of the strength and enthusiasm of our work will lie in a consciousness of the fact that although we may be strangers to each other we are nevertheless all working *together* and for a *common purpose.*

Purpose of the League

As the work has progressed during the months past the objects toward which we need to labor have been growing more and more distinct.

1. Our one supreme object is to raise the tone of our citizenship. The city will not become permanently better except as we who live in the city become better. There are large sections of our town that yield to the guidance of corrupt and designing men for the reason that they are unreached by influences of a finer and more generous kind. Plans are being formulated by which we expect to come into touch with some such portions of the city, and your coöperation in this work will soon be solicited.

2. We need to become better acquainted with the machi-

nery of our city government and with certain principles and statutes by which the motion of that machinery requires to be regulated. Each subsequent bulletin will contain one or two samples of such statutes. We cannot criticize our public servants except as we are familiar with the laws to which they are properly amenable.

3. In order to a complete grasp upon the situation we require to be acquainted with certain facts relating to the present condition of the city. This and succeeding bulletins will contain certain questions bearing upon your own election district. The answers to such questions will none of them involve much labor on your part, but in course of time will aggregate a large amount of valuable information. (In this connection it is suggested that further labor upon the map of your district be postponed until such facts as it may be thought best to use have been collected, after which the map can be prepared by yourself, or at the central office, as you may prefer.)

Questions

Please forward to your Assembly-district supervisor, as below, within two weeks from date, answers to the following questions:

1. How is your district bounded?
2. Is your district occupied by residences, stores, offices, or manufactories?
3. How many public-school buildings are there in your district, and where located?
4. How many saloons are there in the district?

Yours truly,

........................,

Supervisor............*Assembly District.*

BULLETIN NO. 2.

FEBRUARY, 1893.

DEAR SIR: At the meeting of the executive committee just held reports were received from the Assembly districts already occupied, showing encouraging growth in membership and a cordial entrance upon the work in hand. One such district has taken the initiative in developing an organization among its own election-district men, and a sub-committee of the executive committee has been designated to report at the next meeting a plan of Assembly-district organization. Work has just been commenced in one new Assembly district and a quarter of its election districts already supplied with men.

Information.—Any person, licensed or otherwise, who shall sell or offer for sale or give away any strong or spirituous liquors, wines, ale, or beer on Sunday; or on any other day between one and five o'clock in the morning, unless he have a special license therefor; or to any child actually or apparently under the age of sixteen years, or to any intoxicated person, shall be guilty of a misdemeanor.

Except to parties already licensed no new license can be granted for the sale of liquor in any building (other than a hotel, or building for which a license already exists) which shall be on the same street or avenue and within two hundred feet of a building occupied exclusively as a church or school-house; measurements to be taken between the principal entrances of the buildings in question.

The Board of Excise, whose office is at 54 Bond Street, is required to keep a record showing the name of such licensee, the locality of the premises licensed, and the date of granting license. Such record-book is required to be open to the inspection of the public.

Recommendation.—It is recommended that each member of the League should go provided with a note-book, in which record shall be made of any fact or incident coming to his knowledge which connects itself with the purposes of the League and the administration of our municipal government.

Caution.—Members are advised not to publish the fact of their membership. It is also entirely foreign to the spirit and purpose of the League that any parties should be questioned upon matters of their own private concern.

Questions

5. As you come to understand better your own district what is *the* evil existing there which seems to you particularly to require correction?

6. Please give street and number of any saloons that may exist in your district.

7. What saloons have you, if any, which are situated within two hundred feet of a church or school-house?

8. Have you any churches in your district, and, if so, where are they situated, and of what denomination?

9. Is there any special point upon which you would like to have the law stated or information given in a later bulletin?

N.B.—Please fill out these blanks, retaining one yourself for future reference and returning the other within two weeks to
Yours truly,

........................,

Supervisor............*Assembly District.*

NEW YORK, February 15, 1893.

BULLETIN NO. 3.

DEAR SIR: At the March meeting of the executive committee, held on the 2d inst., a committee chosen at the previous meeting to consider the matter of Assembly-district organization reported a plan for such organization, and their report was adopted. One Assembly district organized in accordance with that plan the evening following, and others are expecting to do so in the course of the present month. In this way Leaguers will be drawn into closer relation to each other, and our work therefore be made easier, more interesting, and more productive.

It is part of the purpose of the League to interest itself in all those matters which concern the weal of the city in its different portions, and accordingly at our March meeting a committee was chosen to consider the "sweating" business as it is conducted in the southeasterly districts, and, if possible, to effect some arrangement with the "anti-sweaters" there resident by which we can work with them to the repression of this vicious system of industrial slavery. As the League becomes strengthened and solidified other matters of similar importance will be taken up in other portions of the city.

Information.—POLICE JUSTICES.—There are in the city fifteen police justices, appointed by the mayor for a term of ten years, and receiving each an annual salary of $8000. The labors of these justices are divided as follows:

Three to hold the Court of Special Sessions;
Two at the Tombs;   Two at Fifty-seventh Street;
Two at Essex Market;   Two at Harlem;
Two at Jefferson Market;   Two at Morrisania.

DUTIES OF POLICEMAN.—"It shall be a misdemeanor, punishable by imprisonment in the penitentiary for not less than one year, nor exceeding two years, or by a fine of not less than $250, for any member of the police force to wilfully neglect making any arrest for an offense against the law of this State or ordinance in force in the city of New York."—*Section* 280, *Act of Consolidation.*

Reminder.—No Leaguer who reports violation of law thereby runs any risk of being called to testify upon the matter on the witness-stand.

Questions

10. If there are any saloons in your district will you report whether they are licensed, and, if so, when do their licenses expire?

NOTE.—In order to gain this information your best way will be to go to the rooms of the Board of Excise, 54 Bond Street, and ask for the record-book which covers the particular police precinct in which your saloons are located. This will be put in your hands, and in it you will be able easily, by knowing the street and number where the saloon is situated, to discover whether the keeper is credited with a license, and, if so, when the license expires. There is also a record kept at the station-house, but that you will not probably be allowed to consult. If you do not know the number of your police precinct, you can learn it by inquiring of your Assembly-district supervisor, or by writing to the secretary of the City Vigilance League.

11. Are there in your election district any residences, apartment-houses, tenement-houses, or saloons, the name of the owner of which you are able to state? If so, will you please give street and number, with name of owner so far as you are able to do so *confidently?*

12. Are there any portions of your election district that have been conspicuously neglected by the so-called street-cleaning department during the past two months?

13. Please report any item of special interest or importance which occurs to you in connection with the purposes of the League, or any incident which it would be well for us to know which has fallen under your observation and which has to do with the interests of our city.

N.B.—Please fill out these blanks, retaining one copy for your own future reference and returning the other within two weeks to

Yours truly,

........................,

Supervisor............*Assembly District.*

NEW YORK, March 17, 1893.

BULLETIN NO. 4.

Dear Sir: Reports made to the executive committee at their April meeting showed that in the Assembly districts where work has been begun the ranks of supervisors are being filled up (three such districts having already nearly their full complement). Progress is also being made in the matter of organizing Assembly-district workers. This matter is urged upon the attention of Assembly leaders. Each election-district man needs to have his own field and to feel his particular responsibility for it; at the same time, in order to do his best work, he needs also to feel a degree of responsibility for the entire Assembly district, and that cannot be the case till he and the other workers in the same Assembly district have come into relation with each other and been organized. With that accomplished they can then, under the direction of the Assembly leader, consider and mature plans looking to the interests of the whole Assembly district. This will brighten and solidify our work and make it easier and more intelligent.

Trouble at the Excise Office.—We are not surprised to learn that the treatment which the supervisors have received at the rooms of the Board of Excise, No. 54 Bond Street, is reported to have been more or less inhospitable. Tammany will resent all disposition on our part to watch its operations. That is one great reason why the City Vigilance League exists. We may have something additional to say upon the matter, but in this bulletin will only give two or three facts in relation to the board with which we ought all to be familiar, and will also state the provision of the law which entitles us to inspect its records.

The Board of Excise.—The board is at present [1893] constituted as follows: W. S. Andrews (president), Leicester Holme, W. Dalton. Excise commissioners are appointed by the mayor for a term of three years, with an annual salary of $5000. The term of office of the present commissioners will expire April 30, 1895.

The Records of the Excise Board are Public Property.— " Every Board of Excise shall keep a book of minutes in which shall be entered every resolution passed by it granting or refusing a license, and a complete record of all other proceedings of the board. Every Board of Excise shall also keep a record-book showing in separate columns the name of each licensee, the locality of the premises licensed, the character and class of each license, the date of granting the same, the amount of the license fee, the date of the payment thereof, and the name and residence of each surety on the bond of each licensee. *Each book of minutes and record-book of every Board of Excise shall be open to the inspection of the public* when not necessarily in use by the board, and if of a Board of Excise of a city shall be kept at its office, and if of a Board of Excise of a town shall be kept in the office of the town clerk of the town."—*Chapter* 401, *Section* 12, *of the Laws of* 1892.

Answers to Questions

1. The president and executive committee of the League pledge themselves to summon no supervisor to testify in court because of any statement he may have made or information he may have given.

2. Responsibility of owner or agent of property for gambling or disorderly conduct on the premises. The law upon this is as follows:

" A person who keeps a room, shed, tenement, etc., . . . to be used for gambling, . . . or, *being the owner or agent*, knowingly lets or permits the same to be so used, is guilty of a misdemeanor."—*Penal Code, Section* 343.

" A person who keeps a house of ill fame, or assignation of any description, . . . or who, *as agent or owner*, lets a building or any portion of a building, knowing that it is intended to be used for any purpose specified in this section, or who permits a building or portion of a building to be so used, is guilty of a misdemeanor."—*Penal Code, Section* 322.

Questions

14. Are you aware of the existence in your district of any gambling-houses or policy-shops, and, if so, where are they located?

15. Are the streets in your district showing the effect of the criticism which has been passed by community upon the man who is drawing salary as commissioner of the department of street-cleaning?

16. When you went to 54 Bond Street to inquire in regard to the saloons in your district what kind of treatment did you receive?

17. If you are a Democrat do you think it important that the mayor of this city should be a Democrat? Or if you are a Republican do you think it important that he should be a Republican? In other words: Do you think we need anything else in a mayor than that he should be an honest man and competent to administer the affairs of the city in a manner to promote its common interests?

18. Can you give the names, confidently, of the owners of any property in your district additional to those which you stated in reply to Bulletin No. 3?

N.B.—Please return this bulletin with questions answered, *at the earliest possible date,* to the undersigned, reserving a duplicate copy for your own future reference.

Yours truly,

........................,

Supervisor............*Assembly District.*

NEW YORK, April 20, 1893.

The administrative methods of the League will be described in detail, because they have proved eminently practical and can be used in other cities with only a slight change necessitated by local conditions. In the first place, the membership is kept on cards, on the principle of the card catalogue. One name is placed on each card and the following data filled in:

Assembly................ *Election*..................

Name ....

Address { *Office*..............................
{ *House*..............................

Occupation..

Church ....

Denomination ....

Society..

Remarks:

....

....

The *society* refers to one like the Christian Endeavor, the Epworth League, and the various others. The fact regarding *occupation* is of value, in order that the secretary may select a man who is capable of responding to just the demand placed upon him. These facts are for the use of the secretary and the executive committee.

At the various meetings held under the auspices of the League members are recruited by means of pledge-cards, which are directed on the reverse side to the secretary. By means of such cards the enthusiasm which is aroused at a meeting crystallizes into something definite when the name is signed, and then the recruit is placed under the oversight of the local leader.

THE CITY VIGILANCE LEAGUE

NEW YORK CITY

Our sole aim is to raise the tone of citizenship. Whatever concerns the welfare of our city is made the subject of our inquiry and conference.

All citizens are cordially invited to become Associate Members of the League. The conditions of membership are recognized sympathy with its objects and the payment of an annual fee of *not less than* $3, which will include subscription to the *City Vigilant*, the monthly publication of the League.

I hereby apply for membership.
I desire to be classed as an Active Member (no dues).
I desire to be classed as an Associate Member.

(Erase one of the last two sentences.)

Name ....

Residence { *House* ....
{ *Office* ....

Your name will be forwarded by the secretary to your supervisor, who will then communicate with you.

Assembly Dist. ....*Election* ....

In order that the new member may feel that he is looked after by the League and is not swallowed up in a great organization, he receives a notice from the secretary to the effect that his name has been received. By this means his individuality is retained. This note is sent to each new member:

"It gives me pleasure to acknowledge your application for active associate membership in the City Vigilance League. I have placed your name on the roll and have also forwarded it to the proper League official for his information. Associate membership entitles you to our organ, the *City Vigilant*, which will be duly sent you each month.

"Your residence determines your enrolment in the....... Assembly District, of which municipal area............... ....is the chairman of the local League organization.

" 'The objects of this League shall be to quicken among its members an appreciation of their municipal obligations; to acquaint them with existing conditions; to familiarize them with the machinery of municipal government; to make conspicuous the respects in which such government is languidly or criminally administered; to regard with jealous concern the point at which private interest enters into competition with the general good; and in every possible way to repress in the community what makes for its detriment, and to foster whatsoever seems fitted to promote its advantage.

" 'This League aims to accomplish its objects by the collection and dissemination of full and accurate data concerning our municipal conditions; by legislation; by legal proceedings; by the hearty support of officials who discharge their duties faithfully, and the vigorous prosecution of those who neglect them; and by the creation of a public sentiment in furtherance of the objects of the League.'

"In accordance with the above statements from the League constitution it will give me pleasure to hear from you on any phase of municipal life which you think should be made the subject of inquiry or conference."

It is not enough that the new member be notified, but at the same time the local leader is sent this letter:

"*Chairman of........Assembly.*

"DEAR SIR: I send you the name of

....

"Address $\begin{cases} \text{Office} \ldots\ldots\ldots\ldots\ldots\ldots\ldots\ldots\ldots\ldots\ldots \\ \text{House} \ldots\ldots\ldots\ldots\ldots\ldots\ldots\ldots\ldots\ldots\ldots \end{cases}$

Recommended by ....

He has applied for active associate membership, and his residence as above determines his enrolment in your Assembly. While no work is expected from the associate members it is deemed advisable that you should know those residing in your district.

"If an applicant for active membership is not recommended by any one please satisfy yourself that he will fill the requirements for League membership.

"Please return this slip, with the following information concerning active members, for the use of the secretary:

Occupation..

Church..

Denomination...

Society ....

Assembly......Election......Ward......Precinct......

"The object of the above information is to enable us to call on certain members for that kind of work for which their profession fits them. Each new member, whether active or associate, has been informed in what Assembly district he has been enrolled and that you are the chairman of the League organization in that district; hence you should feel no hesitancy in calling on the active members for any coöperation. It is suggested that you devise some method by which a portion of the responsibility for the local League work in your district may be placed on the shoulders of each new active member, in order that he may be aware that he is a member of something."

In its investigations it became necessary for the League to concern itself with the observance of the Sunday excise law. It was also desired to locate the saloons in the various districts, in order to be informed of their exact number. In voluntary work it has been found that the most careful instructions will yield a great diversity of results, so that in the tabulation of a great number of reports the labor is increased many fold because the reports are not uniform. To obviate this unnecessary labor, and to make it as easy as possible for the Leaguers, diagrams of each block were prepared, with the definite questions. This scheme has proved very satisfactory.

The League realizes that a lack of system in tabulating ascertained facts greatly impairs the usefulness of the study in question. The pictorial features of Charles Booth's studies in London are of great value. The League therefore proposes to prepare maps of each Assembly district, on which will be indicated its civic characteristics. By this means the location of the lodging-houses will be indicated, and it will be very easy to note the sections of the city selected by them. The same plan can be followed in the case of churches, schools, saloons, and tenement-houses.

THE CITY VIGILANCE LEAGUE

PLEASE CHECK THE APPROXIMATE LOCATION IN THE BLOCK BY AN X.

..........*Assembly Dist.* ....*blocks.*
..........*Election Dist.*
..........*Ward*
..........*Police Precinct*
Captain..

Date..

Saloons.................... *Churches*.................... *Schools*....................

1..
2..
3..
4..
5..
6..
7..
8..
9..
10...

PLEASE FILL IN NAME AND ADDRESS OF SALOONS.

For the sake of coördinating the work and preventing overlapping of effort the activities of the League are divided into the following departments. At the head of each is a member of the executive committee. By this means the executive committee, which meets regularly each month, is conversant with the entire management, and any new item of business is referred at once to its appropriate committee.

PUBLICATIONS
- *The City Vigilant* (monthly), $1 per year.
- "*The Handbook of Sociological References*," price $1.10.

Legal Aid.
Finance.
League Affiliation.
Conferences.
Education.
Lecture Bureau.
Excise: Saloon Substitute No. 1.
Tenement-houses.
Lodging-houses.
Labor.
Membership and Organization.
Baths and Lavatories.

These departments are self-explanatory, but the work of the Legal Aid—one of the most important—must be described in detail. Already very many worthy cases have been brought to the knowledge of this committee, with the result that justice has been secured. It is not the aim that this department shall be a charity, for in each case a fee is requested, in order that the recipient of the legal aid may still retain his independence. This committee is also a kind of "consulting attorney" for the general secretary, in securing legal information to answer various inquiries.

CITY VIGILANCE LEAGUE

DEPARTMENT OF LEGAL AID

New York,..................1895.

Mr........................

Dear Sir: The following case is referred to your committee, with the request that you render such services therein to the applicant as may be required.

Yours truly,

....

President.

Statement of Case.

Name of Applicant..

Residence..

Occupation..

Business Address..

References..

Nature of Complaint.....................................

Against Whom...

Remarks..

Mr.................,

Of Counsel to Legal Aid Committee.

DEAR SIR: Please take charge of the foregoing case and report the result of your action therein.

Yours very truly,
C. A. B. PRATT,
Chairman Legal Aid Committee,
111 *Broadway.*

NEW YORK,.................1895.

The first public meeting under the auspices of the League was held in Chickering Hall, April 20, 1894, in the interest of good municipal government. The crowded audience evinced the public interest in the speakers and in the subjects that were discussed. After the League had made its *début*, it was the feeling that a public testimonial, in the shape of a complimentary dinner, to its president, Dr. Parkhurst, would be a fitting recognition of his public services, and would also show who in the community would dare to indorse the movement which he represented by attending the dinner. The result was most gratifying, for nearly two hundred men from all walks of life came out to do him honor. Charles Stewart Smith, the then president of the Chamber of Commerce, presided, with James C. Carter, Colonel A. S. Bacon, and others as speakers. Avowed support in those days, when there was so much anonymous sympathy, and before the movement had succeeded, was doubly acceptable. Two letters received on that occasion will illustrate the above point:

"NEW YORK, April 13, 1894.

"DEAR SIR: I am in receipt of your very kind letter of the 11th instant, extending to me an invitation to the complimentary dinner to be given to Rev. Dr. Parkhurst on April 30th.

Nothing would give me greater pleasure than to participate in this testimonial of esteem to Dr. Parkhurst, on account of my admiration for his indefatigable zeal and fearless conduct, and my deep sympathy with the good work in which he is engaged; but as I shall have to be in Washington on the day of the dinner, for the purpose of presiding over the Annual Congress, National Society Sons of the American Revolution, I will be compelled to forego the pleasure of accepting your polite invitation.

"With many regrets, I am

"Yours truly,

[Signed] "HORACE PORTER.

"WILLIAM HOWE TOLMAN, *Secretary*,
"New York City."

"NEW YORK, April 16, 1894.

"DEAR SIR: I am exceedingly sorry that it is impossible for me to be present at the complimentary dinner to be tendered to Dr. Charles H. Parkhurst, April 30th. I should be very sorry if my absence counted as an indication of lukewarmness or indifference. There is no braver man in America than Dr. Parkhurst, and the Civil War itself brought out no greater illustration of heroism than he has illustrated. A wedding engagement that evening makes it impossible for me to be present; though so anxious am I to witness my loyal support of Dr. Parkhurst that if I find it possible to reach the hotel even as late as ten o'clock I shall do so.

"Yours respectfully,

[Signed] "LYMAN ABBOTT.

"MR. EDWIN S. KASSING."

The result of the November election, in which the majority of the voters declared themselves for good government, is well known. That victory the League considers as one more guide-board pointing out the road toward permanency in good government, for it well knows that one victory does not end the campaign. On the day after election Dr. Parkhurst sent this letter to the various League leaders:

"No. 133 East Thirty-fifth Street,
New York, November 7, 1894.

"I take this early opportunity of congratulating you, as the leader of your district, upon the splendid work which the League has just been doing and the overwhelming results which have followed. While we are not blind to the fact of the immense amount of work which has been done by affiliated organizations, we remember together this morning the long and trying thirty months through which we have been laboring together, and laboring, too, for a large part of that time, when the current of opinion was so strongly against us. Such fidelity ought not to go unrecognized.

"We have come now, not to the end, but rather to the beginning of our efforts. This victory lays for us a foundation upon which we can go on to build with largest hope and assurance."

Enough has been said to indicate the general policy of the League; hence the work in the coming years will be a deepening of those principles of non-sectarianism and non-partizanship which have been so successful in winning for it the confidence and the support of the community.

The administrative offices of the League are in the United Charities Building, 105 East Twenty-second Street. The friends of the League have shown their practical interest in its affairs by their contributions to the Memorial Fund. By this means a permanent home has been provided, where its work will be centered and whence its sphere of usefulness will be extended. The officials of the League are: C. H. Parkhurst, D.D., president; W. H. P. Faunce, D.D., Hon. Abram S. Hewitt, A. E. Kittredge, D.D., Rt. Rev. Henry C. Potter, James A. Scrymser, Charles Stewart Smith, Josiah Strong, D.D., vice-presidents; William Howe Tolman, Ph.D., secretary; William M. Kingsley, treasurer.

www.ingramcontent.com/pod-product-compliance
Lightning Source LLC
Chambersburg PA
CBHW031829230426
43669CB00009B/1284